Manufacturing in America:

A Legacy of Excellence

Manufacturing in America:

A Legacy of Excellence

by Robert Muccigrosso and Ceila Dame Robbins

Douglas R. Kurkul, Executive Editor and Project Director

GREENWICH PUBLISHING GROUP, INC.
LYME, CONNECTICUT

The Timken Roller Bearing Axle Co., 1902; above, Amgen, Inc., 1990s

Produced and published by Greenwich Publishing Group, Inc.
Lyme, Connecticut

Design by Clare Cunningham Graphic Design
Essex, Connecticut

Separation & film assembly by Silver Eagle Graphics, Inc.

Manufacturing in America: A Legacy of Excellence is sponsored by Tenneco Inc. and Case Corporation, with additional support from Ingersoll-Rand Company. The text paper used in this book is 100# Celesta gloss and the dust jacket is 80# C-1-S, both of which were donated by Westvaco Corporation, New York, New York. The binding cloth is trade book black, natural finish, and was donated by Industrial Coatings Group, Inc., Chicago, Illinois. Stamping dies were furnished by Owasso Graphic Arts, Owasso, Michigan. Printing and binding were donated by Worzalla Publishing Company, Inc., Stevens Point, Wisconsin.

Library of Congress Cataloging-in-Publication Data

Muccigrosso, Robert
     Manufacturing in America: A Legacy of Excellence / by Robert Muccigrosso and Ceila Dame Robbins
       p. cm.
       Includes index.
       ISBN 0-944641-15-6 (alk. paper)
       1. United States — Manufacturers — History. 2. Quality of products — United States — History. I. Robbins, Ceila Dame. II. Title.
    HD9725.M83 1995
    338.4'767 — dc20   95-38734
                              CIP

First Printing: October 1995

10 9 8 7 6 5 4 3 2 1

THE MANUFACTURING INSTITUTE

MANUFACTURING MAKES AMERICA STRONG

The Manufacturing Institute is the educational and research affiliate of the National Association of Manufacturers (NAM). The Manufacturing Institute is a 501(c)(3) tax-exempt organization, and all funds are contributed by corporations, associations and foundations.

The principal activity of The Manufacturing Institute, The Manufacturing Campaign, was launched in 1991 as a multi-year educational initiative by the NAM. Its mission is to promote a pro-manufacturing, pro-growth agenda in Washington and across the country. Throughout 1995, The Manufacturing Institute is helping the NAM celebrate 100 years of manufacturing excellence. *Manufacturing in America: A Legacy of Excellence* is one of the highlights of this public outreach campaign. In addition, The Manufacturing Institute provides funds for educational programs, public opinion research, plant tours, scholarly papers and more.

Contact The Manufacturing Institute at (202) 637-3108 for more information on its programs and activities.

Jerry J. Jasinowski	Chairman
Ladd K. Biro	President
Douglas R. Kurkul	Executive Editor and Project Director
Mark Robbins	Executive Director, Operations

NAM National Association of Manufacturers

The National Association of Manufacturers (NAM) is the nation's oldest and largest broad-based industrial trade association. Its more than 13,500 member companies and subsidiaries — including 10,000 small manufacturers — are located in every state and produce approximately 85 percent of US manufactured goods. Through its member companies and affiliated associations, the NAM represents every industrial sector, 185,000 businesses and more than 18 million employees.

The NAM's mission is to enhance the competitiveness of manufacturers by shaping a legislative and regulatory environment conducive to US economic growth in a global economy, and to increase understanding among policymakers, the media and the general public about the importance of manufacturing to America's economic strength and standard of living.

Founded 190 years ago in Cincinnati, the NAM is proud to celebrate its centennial in 1995.

The NAM is headquartered in Washington, D.C., and has regional offices across the nation.

A listing of the owners of all trademarked names used in this book may be found on page 160. While every effort has been made to correctly identify all trademark owners, the publisher apologizes in advance for any unintentional errors or omissions. We welcome any corrections on company letterhead and will insert the appropriate acknowledgment in subsequent editions of this book. Please contact Greenwich Publishing Group, Inc., 243 Hamburg Road, Lyme, CT 06371.

Table of Contents

Foreword   6

Introduction   8

Chapter One   10
Manufacturers Unite to Sell to the World (1890 - 1900)

Chapter Two   24
Industry Meets the Needs of a Growing World Power (1901 - 1919)

Chapter Three   40
Business Booms During the Jazz Age (1920 - 1929)

Chapter Four   56
The Great Depression Tests Ingenuity (1930 - 1940)

Chapter Five   68
Manufacturing Helps Win the War (1941 - 1945)

Chapter Six   86
Peacetime Prosperity and New Conflicts (1946 - 1960)

Chapter Seven   102
Information Alters an Age (1961 - 1980)

Chapter Eight   116
Modern Challenges and Opportunities (1981-Present)

Epilogue   132
American Manufacturing Meets the Global Challenge

Acknowledgments   134

Timeline   136

National Industrial Council and Associations Council Members   156

Index   158

Credits   160

Foreword

The history of manufacturing in the United States is one of the world's great economic success stories. Given the advantages of a resource-rich continent, ample capital, an expanding labor supply and the protection of two oceans, it is easy to conclude that America's development into an industrial colossus was inevitable.

It was not. Britain did not intend that its wilderness colony industrialize; its role was to supply raw materials to British industry and captive markets for its products. Laws forbade trade between the American colonies and other countries and prohibited many types of manufacturing.

Yet the power of individual initiative that Adam Smith wrote about in *The Wealth of Nations*, published the same year Thomas Jefferson wrote the Declaration of Independence, took hold in America. One of the New World's earliest industrialists, an English immigrant named Samuel Slater, built machines for the manufacture of cloth entirely from memory — because it was a crime to carry factory plans out of England.

In the subsequent years of America's industrial development, thousands of similar stories unfolded: the cloth peddler who sold denim to California gold miners (The Levi Strauss Co.); the teenager who sold pickles door to door (H.J. Heinz Co.); the Atlanta pharmacist who concocted a new soft drink (Coca-Cola); and the young man who hocked his car to raise money to manufacture the computer he co-designed (Apple Computer).

These kinds of stories are by no means confined to the past. They are still unfolding as new industries are invented in backyard garages and old ones re-invented in high-rise corporate offices.

Today the advent of the microchip is ushering in a new phase of America's economic development, known variously as the Information Age or Knowledge Economy.

This new era is likened to the transition of America from the agrarian economy envisioned by Jefferson to Mark Twain's "booming bustling" industrial economy of the late 19th century.

One hundred years ago, the output of America's factories first began to exceed the output of America's farms. Yet this did not portend the demise of agriculture. In fact, today American agriculture leads the world in both total production and productivity and remains a key sector of our economy.

Similarly, America's transition to a knowledge economy does not mean the decline of manufacturing. Manufacturing retains a remarkably consistent share of our total output and supports large segments of the service economy. Our industrial sector is the world's largest, produces more than it ever has and leads the world in exports. It also has the world's highest level of productivity, which means that it will continue to support the well-paying jobs that are critical to our traditionally high living standards.

Manufacturing's legacy of excellence, aptly cited in the title of this book, is itself a legacy — of an imperfect yet enormously powerful system of economic organization known as capitalism that is only just beginning to capture the wealth-creating potential of humankind.

To those who doubt that potential, consider the stunning proportions of our growth: In the past 50 years we have added over seven times as much to the world's producing power as was added during all the previous millennia of organized society. This fact alone gives us cause for optimism as we exit one century and enter another.

Dana G. Mead
Chairman & Chief Executive Officer, Tenneco Inc.
Chairman, National Association of Manufacturers
October 1995

Introduction

O n May 1, 1893, Chicago opened the gates to the World's Columbian Exposition. For the 25 million visitors who came to marvel at the wonders of science, industry and art on display, it was a gateway to the future.

The exposition gave people a vision of the incredible possibilities that lay ahead — and Americans thrilled at the prospect. Central to the spectacle was the magic of electricity, which bathed the "White City" in light, powered the elevated train that circled the fairground and worked the newfangled tools and home appliances on display.

The gargantuan Manufactures and Liberal Arts Building, which rose to an equivalent height of 19 stories, housed everything from furniture to carpet sweepers to fire alarms, providing, as one historian has noted, "a cornucopia of material culture that not only catered to middle-class taste but helped to form that taste."

In the Woman's Building, visitors were tantalized by the model kitchen and mechanical household devices that would take hours off the tedious routines of domestic tasks.

From the towering Ferris Wheel to the tiny teeth of the early zippers on display, the exposition dazzled viewers. It was bright; it was grand; and, most of all, it offered incredible promise for the future.

In the next 100 years, America's industries delivered on that promise. The early stoves, dishwashers, phonographs, cameras and telephones became usable, affordable products that gave the average person an unprecedented standard of living and leisure. They were followed by new technologies that brought products and

Lithograph by an unknown artist

possibilities that existed only on the farthest edges of fantasy in 1893.

When the exposition opened, the processes were already underway that would bring that glorious future to life. In 1893, the nation was in the midst of a dramatic shift from an agrarian to an industrial society and from a manufacturing system that made goods a few at a time to one that mass produced them in astounding quantities. Behind the transformation were new transportation and communication systems that united the country, new sources of energy, technological innovations in manufacturing — and the sheer energy and inventiveness of the people who developed the country's industries.

In the years that have passed since the World's Columbian Exposition, manufacturing has profoundly changed the way Americans live — the way they work, play, travel, communicate, learn, eat and almost every other aspect of their existence. This is the story of the people, products and processes that have changed lives — and are still changing them today.

Lithograph after a painting by Charles Graham

THE FERRIS WHEEL
MIDWAY PLAISANCE
WORLD'S COLUMBIAN EXPOSITION
· CHICAGO 1893 ·

HIGHEST LINE OF VISION, 258 feet.
HIGHEST POINT OF WHEEL, 264 feet.
DIAMETER OF WHEEL, (center of pins,) 250 feet.
TOTAL WEIGHT OF WHEEL AND CARS, 2100 tons.
TOTAL WEIGHT OF PEOPLE PER TRIP, only 150 tons.

TIME REQUIRED FOR ONE TRIP, 20 minutes.
DUPLICATE REVERSING ENGINES, 1000 horse power each.
TOTAL WEIGHT of wheel, levers and machinery, 4300 tons.
CARRYING CAPACITY, 36 CARS,

Detail of *The Ironworkers' Noontime* by Thomas Pollock Anshutz; opposite page, Campbell's Soup labels past and present

CHAPTER ONE

Manufacturers Unite to Sell to the World

1 8 9 0 – 1 9 0 0

Alexander Hamilton, the nation's first secretary of the treasury, issued an insightful *Report on Manufactures* to the United States Congress in 1791. Concerned with the nation's debt, dearth of foreign trade and overwhelming dependence on agriculture, he argued for the need to foster manufacturing in order to promote growth, security and overall well-being. Some considered his vision too radical for their time.

The nineteenth century proved Hamilton's critics wrong. Many came to realize that his *Report* represented, in the words of one historian, "the grand design by which the United States became the greatest industrial power in the world." Economic and technological expansion, especially in the years after the Civil War, propelled the nation to new heights and drew worldwide admiration. From the McCormick reaper to the telephone, manufacturing played a pivotal role in society's advances. By the early 1890s, lumber mills, brick-yards, iron and steel factories, flour mills and farm-machinery makers were prospering. Many U.S. cities had become major manufacturing centers.

The World's Columbian Exposition of 1893 gave expression to the nation's achievements and aspirations as could no other event in those times. Not least among the marvels of the exposition was the gigantic Manufactures and Liberal Arts Building, whose frame consumed more than twice as much iron and steel as did the Brooklyn Bridge. It was the largest building in the world, but size alone did not make it a focal point of the exposition.

Visitors thronged to the building to gaze at the sheer volume of the new machinery and gadgetry, as well as a massive department store that displayed a stunning assortment of the latest in consumer wares. Along with a host of other scientific and mechanical wonders displayed at the Chicago fair that summer — including the dramatic use of electricity to light the grounds during the evenings — the beguilements of the Manufactures and Liberal Arts Building spoke to what American industry had accomplished, was accomplishing and promised to accomplish.

As the Columbian Exposition approached its end, however, the nation sank into a severe depression (or "panic," as it was then termed). American Federation of Labor President Samuel Gompers called it "the greatest industrial depression this country has ever witnessed." In all, more than 160,000 businesses failed, the greatest number for any 10-year period since the birth of the republic. Prices fell, debts increased and went unpaid, and unemployment soared.

Manufacturers recognized that expanded trade in foreign markets, especially the newer ones of Asia and Latin America, might substantially alleviate their predicament. Spurred on by this vision and by the suggestion of a southern trade paper called *Dixie*, more than 500 businessmen gathered in Cincinnati in late January 1895 to form the National Association of Manufacturers of the United States of America — their goal: to augment both foreign and domestic commerce. The depression ended within two years, and foreign trade more than doubled within the next five. By 1900, the United States exported more manufactured products than raw materials. Meanwhile, the NAM itself was growing, particularly in the area of export promotion, and helping the manufacturing sector to speed the United States into the twentieth century.

Founding of the National Association of Manufacturers

During the 1890s, the United States sought to increase its foreign trade, especially with the largely untapped markets of Asia and Latin America. This goal gained urgency from the depression that began in 1893, which caused the ruin of more than 360 banks in a six-month period and brought unemployment levels up to 20 percent of the industrial labor force by the winter of 1893-94. Manufacturers hoping to export faced an array of obstacles.

On the weekend of January 22, 1895, business executives from across the country convened in Cincinnati to establish an organization to represent industry in both trade and domestic matters. Ohio Governor William McKinley addressed the convention and the Queen City gave the delegates a warm welcome. The 583 participants of the inaugural meeting of this "National Association of Manufacturers" elected Thomas Dolan, a Philadelphia businessman, as its first president. Soon thereafter, the organization began lobbying for such matters as reciprocal trade agreements, an improved U.S. Merchant Marine, the construction of a canal through Central America and a federal department to foster commerce. The NAM also provided personalized trade assistance: from a tour of Argentina and Brazil, to warehouses in Europe and China. From 1895 to 1900, exports of U.S. manufactured goods rose from $183 million to $433 million.

National Industrial Review cover, April 1895

Niagara Falls and the Promise of Electricity

Already a mecca for tourists, Niagara Falls became the site of the nation's first large hydroelectric power plant in 1895. Electric power seemed to be the biggest boost to industry since the steam engine that had started the industrial revolution nearly 100 years earlier. Most of the electric power was produced by steam- or water-powered generators. Not only were water-powered generators cleaner than wood- and coal-burning steam engines, electrical power could be transferred and connected to many different machines without a complicated and dangerous network of cogs and gears.

Prominent experts — Thomas A. Edison among them — generally advocated direct current for transmitting electrical power. Though Edison's original criticism of alternating current threatened to diminish the possibilities it presented, Nikola Tesla's experiments with alternating current launched a revolution in the uses for electricity. Tesla eventually proved the benefits and safety of alternating current — sometimes by letting the electricity flow through his own body.

The Niagara Falls power plant was built by the Westinghouse Electric Company for the Cataract Construction Company, formed by William K. Vanderbilt and J. P. Morgan. The Niagara generator produced alternating current, which could be more economically transmitted over long distances than could lower-voltage direct current. The plant provided inexpensive electricity to the city of Buffalo, a major manufacturing area, 22 miles away.

Increased access to electric power at the turn of the century stimulated the growth of business and industry

and began to ease the tasks of daily life. Factories, no longer limited by proximity to water, increasingly turned to electric motors as cost-cutting measures to achieve greater productivity. The machine tool industry, for one, introduced electrical tools, power presses and compressed air tools. In many other industries, processes that had been run by mechanical devices became faster and more efficient as they came to rely on electrical components.

New industries sprang up to provide the equipment needed for products and processes powered by electricity. For instance, Emerson Electric Co. was formed in 1890 with a small-order benchwork approach to electric motor manufacturing. Over the years, the company adopted progressively more sophisticated and automated manufacturing processes: today the diversified global corporation is the world's leading manufacturer of electric motors.

As electric generating plants and distribution systems were established, the overall effect was to accelerate the growth of industry and increase its productivity.

Above, Niagara Falls Power House; left, *Birth of Power* by an unknown artist which symbolized the dawn of hydroelectric power

Steel Changes the American Skyline

The nation's great industrial cities developed in the late nineteenth century as industries, freed by electricity and railroads from the need to be close to rivers and raw materials, chose to locate closer to available labor and to each other's businesses. As the factories prospered, soaring populations in the cities created land shortages and spiraling real estate prices; in the older cities, this overcrowding was quite a serious problem. The skyscraper — the defining shape of the modern city — was the answer to this dilemma.

Major engineering improvements underlay the development of the taller buildings that increasingly filled the skyline. Not least among them was Elisha Graves Otis's invention of a safety brake for elevators. The Bessemer process was another critical breakthrough. Between 1887 and 1944 one-fifth of all the steel produced in the United States (400 million tons) was a product of the Bessemer process, which used cool air, rather than a blast furnace, to purify larger quantities of iron ore more cheaply. This innovation had made steel more affordable and steel-beam construction had already made waves, as bridges throughout the world were built with steel girders.

But the practicality of the steel "skeleton" for tall buildings was made clear only by the increasing utility of the elevator. The first passenger elevator — introduced by the Otis Brothers on March 23, 1857 — could

Reliance Building, shown here in 1960

lift 1,000 pounds at the rate of 40 feet per minute. The elevator's popularity took off with the height of the new buildings.

The extraordinary tensile strength of steel made it possible to build higher without diminishing structural support. William Le Baron Jenney's Home Insurance Building (1884-1885) in Chicago was the first building actually to employ steel beams, but it was another Chicago edifice, the Tacoma Building (1887-1888), by Holabird and Roche, that depended entirely on such beams for its support. The visitors to the 13-story building were carried skyward by five hydraulic Otis Brothers elevators.

The strength of a steel frame also allowed a more open construction, requiring less masonry in the walls. Edward Shanklin's 14-story Reliance Building, a steel frame construction built in Chicago in 1895, paved the way for future skyscrapers with its portal framing and open glass walls. Made possible by a strong steel industry — particularly in Pennsylvania, Ohio and elsewhere — skyscrapers created new working spaces with increased light and better air quality. (Coincidentally, one of the oldest standing skyscrapers is the Sun Building, located across the street from the NAM's headquarters in Washington, D.C.)

Skyscrapers effectively met the challenges urban builders faced, and they met the needs of increasingly larger companies which took up more and more space. Thus, they managed to overcome the initial trepidation of the public and became symbols of a city's power and pride.

Left, a construction worker resting on the steel frame for the Empire State Building, 1930; above, an early Otis Elevator Company advertisement

Disposable Razor Blades Create the Clean-Shaven Look

The idea for a safety razor came to King C. Gillette sometime in 1895 when, fittingly, he was shaving himself and noted that his straight razor was dull — so dull that stropping would not work; it needed honing by a barber or a cutler. Gillette introduced his razor at a time when the pace of life was quickening, and for those who preferred the clean-shaven look, his invention gradually replaced the slower rituals of lathering and shaving with a straight razor or regularly visiting the local barber shop.

Gillette's concept was simple, but its success depended on industry's capacity for mass production. Though the razor itself could be used indefinitely, the blades would be replaced when dull, which meant that users required a steady supply with a consistent quality. This unique product design allowed a novel marketing strategy: Gillette offered the razor to customers at little or no cost but sold blades at a substantial profit. This simple concept — continuing into modern times with cellular telephones and other products — may have been among the first "loss leaders" in mass marketing history. But for sure, the invention made it easy for men to abandon their beards, and the beardless look soon changed the face of the American male.

Kodak Puts a Camera in Every Hand

When amateur photographer George Eastman bought his first set of photography equipment in 1878, he decided to act upon his fervent belief about photography — more people would use cameras if they were easier to operate.

Eastman started his own company and began a series of innovations that would "make the camera as convenient as the pencil." Initially seeking to simplify the cumbersome equipment needed to take a photo, Eastman quickly developed a way to eliminate the coated glass plates on which the images were recorded in favor of coated paper. He invented and marketed the first roll film camera, the Kodak, in 1888 — the name being just one more of his many creations.

By 1900, Eastman had come up with a camera design and roll film that were simple enough for anyone to use. The "Brownie" camera was designed and marketed for children, but was bought by many an amateur, ensuring that the births, vacations, marriages, memories and historical events of the following generations could be recorded easily and permanently by millions of Americans.

Eastman Kodak marketing poster

The Underwood *Standard No. 5.*

Above, Underwood Typewriter Company advertisement, 1926;
right, *The Remington Girl,* 1902

Office Automation Increases Productivity and Accuracy

Automation increasingly became a part of American office life by the late nineteenth century. Before the typewriter and adding machine, most office documents were produced and reproduced by hand, often requiring companies to hire a night shift of employees expressly to make copies. The use of automated office equipment not only made the recording of information speedier, it also enhanced readability.

The first patent for a prototype of the typewriter was issued in England in 1714. Early keyboards were slow and cumbersome and were primarily used by the blind and for embossed writing. Christopher L. Sholes's typewriter, the first practical model, was introduced in 1867 and marketed by Remington in 1874. By 1900 Remington and the Underwood Typewriter Company were the industry leaders in typewriters.

The first modern adding machine, the "Comptometer," made its appearance in 1887, and its use spread throughout the 1890s. Though he was not its inventor, William Seward Burroughs and his company soon assumed industry leadership. The stock ticker, invented in 1867, was one of the first successful examples of printing/typing technology, and ticker-tape soon became part of the American lexicon.

The stock ticker and the adding machine had clear market niches, but the typewriter met with little success initially; the problem — Remington was marketing the machine to the wrong audience. The literary types to whom Remington gave free sample machines — and from whom little support was received in return — mourned the typewriter's attack on what they considered an art — the handwritten letter. Meanwhile, American business was desperately in need of just such a product that could produce easy-to-read documents faster than the scribes of the past. When the typewriter and its awaiting market converged, those who had once decried its introduction changed their tune.

This automation of the workplace did more than spur productivity. It also created a new place in the business world for women. Automated office equipment created a new set of tasks that could be regulated and standardized by the very machines used to complete them. As secretaries and typists, women had new work opportunities, and American business was transformed by the typewriter, which helped one do the work of many and shrunk several hours of work into one.

Above, W. K. Kellogg touring his plant, 1930;
right, early Ralston Purina advertisement

Breakfast in a Box...

During the last decade of the nineteenth century, improved farming, processing and marketing methods brought Americans an increasing choice of new food products that required little preparation and offered both nutrition and convenience.

Even the simplest of foods was taking on an entirely new — even unrecognizable — look. In 1895, W. K. Kellogg, along with his brother Dr. John Harvey Kellogg, dedicated to finding novel ways to produce nutritious foods, processed flaked cereal in the experimental kitchen of the latter's famous sanitarium in Battle Creek, Michigan. Kellogg's Corn Flakes were first sold under the name Sanitas in 1899 via mail to former patients, and by 1906 the Battle Creek Toasted Corn Flake Company was founded by W. K. Kellogg.

The advent of the first flaked cereal began a flood of health food products. C. W. Post, a former patient at Kellogg's Sanitarium, had formed the Postum Cereal Company and had developed a breakfast beverage he called Monk's Brew in the same town in 1894. (This product met with little success until he gave it a new name that is remembered to this day — Postum.) However, it was the introduction of Post Grape Nuts cereal in 1898 that confirmed "breakfast in a box" to be much more than a fad.

For the turn-of-the-century homemaker, packaged cereals were tools of liberation. With workers in a distant factory doing the time-consuming tasks of preparing and combining the ingredients for the foods that went on the breakfast table, one's hours in the kitchen were reduced.

And Convenience in a Can

Grocers' shelves increasingly displayed prepared foods in tin cans and boxes, all produced by U.S. manufacturers. The success of Campbell's Soup, first marketed in 1897, came about through the discovery of a method of manufacturing soup with a lower water content; the resulting "stock" was less expensive to package and ship. By 1905, the production of chef and chemist John Dorrance's creation had risen to 40,000 cases per week from 10 cases per week in 1897. In 1911, when his soup first reached the store shelves in California, it became one of the first products marketed nationally. The line between "homemade" food and manufactured food was diminishing.

The success of these convenient products powered the transformation of prepared foods from a local, seasonal business into an international industry that continues to thrive by offering ever-increasing nutrition and convenience to consumers.

Above, Campbell Soup Company label, early 1900s; right, Campbell's advertisement, 1926

All the rich tomato goodness is in Campbell's Tomato Soup!

12 cents a can

Detail of *The Detroit Industry*, by Diego M. Rivera; opposite page, Bethlehem Steel workers preparing World War I ammunition

CHAPTER TWO

Industry Meets the Needs of a Growing World Power

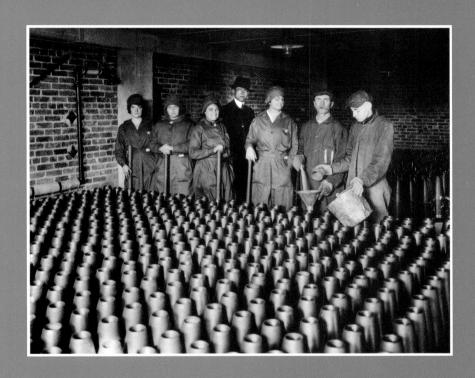

1 9 0 1 - 1 9 1 9

As the twentieth century opened, the United States was already a global economic power. The nation annually produced more than one-half of the world's cotton, corn and oil; more than one-third of its steel, pig iron and silver; and roughly one-third of its coal and gold. Some 6 million of its 75 million inhabitants, or nearly one in twelve, were employed in manufacturing. The engineering profession alone had 136,000 practitioners by 1919, up from 7,000 in 1880. Efficiency was a growing concern, with many manufacturers exploring Frederick Taylor's theory of scientific management. The year 1901 witnessed the organization of United States Steel, the nation's first billion-dollar corporation.

Not everyone applauded the emergence of mammoth corporations. Indeed, the Progressive Era, which lasted from the turn of the century until World War I, provided the setting for political disputes over the optimum size and market power of American businesses. "Bad" trusts existed, argued President Theodore Roosevelt, but so, too, did "good" trusts, ones which provided a variety of needed goods and permitted the United States to compete successfully in world markets. Sometimes forgotten in the debate was the simple fact that the trusts provided many good jobs, leading to higher living standards. Throughout the era, government involvement in and regulation of private industry grew more pronounced.

Meanwhile, manufacturing surged ahead. Established industries like steel, which increasingly was exchanging the Bessemer for the open hearth process, continued to expand; newer ones, such as the automobile — which saw the birth of Henry Ford's assembly line and use of interchangeable parts — grew and inspired others. While not yet a significant factor in the American economy, the airplane, following the successful 1903 flight of the Wright brothers at Kitty Hawk, North Carolina, promised dramatic changes, such as the launch of airmail service in 1918. Less recognized during this era, but similarly portentous, was Robert H. Goddard's initial experimentation with rockets. Corporations' research labs fueled still more innovations.

World War I — the "Great War" as it was called until about 1939 — briefly but crucially interrupted the expansion of domestic manufacturing. Able at first to remain physically distant and unencumbered by Europe's bloodbath, the United States provided impressive amounts of matériel, principally to the Allies. Then in April 1917, Congress acceded to President Woodrow Wilson's call for the nation to participate in "a war to make the world safe for democracy." In somewhat more than a year, over two million American doughboys went "over there" to help defeat the Central Powers. Meanwhile, industry — which drew more heavily upon a work force of women, along with African-Americans who had left the South for northern factories — was providing the tanks, airplanes and equipment needed for victory.

An uncertain peace followed military triumph. The United States Senate refused to ratify the Treaty of Versailles and thereby to join the League of Nations. The "Great Crusade" was over. In the presidential election of 1920, the exhausted American electorate turned to Warren G. Harding, who promised a "return to normalcy."

Mass Production Makes Cars Affordable

Charles and Frank Duryea had begun marketing a gasoline-powered car in 1896. Before the end of the century, Alexander A. Pope's electric cars and the Stanley brothers' steam-driven automobiles were available. At the first National Automobile Show in Madison Square Garden in 1900, these and numerous other "break-through" designs were put on display for the well-dressed crowd. Henry Ford displayed his 1896 model, but it gave little indication of what was to come, for it was his later Model T that made the United States a nation of car fanciers.

The Model T wasn't Ford's first car. Nor was it the first car to have a mass market: Ransom E. Olds sold more than 12,000 Mercury Oldsmobiles in the early 1900s. What then was the critical difference that made the Model T one out of every two cars on the road in 1925? The Model T, intro-duced in 1908, was versatile, rugged and simple, and mass production made it accessible to almost every-one, rather than a high-priced toy for the affluent. Ford didn't invent the assembly line, specialized labor and interchangeable parts, but he improved them significantly, particu-larly by using conveyor belts to create the moving assembly line in 1913. The resulting productivity of his plants is what made the Model T so affordable. True to his vision of a car all of America could buy, Ford passed the savings along to the customer. As a result, the Model T's price actually declined (from $825-$850 in 1908 to $360 in 1916 and $295 in 1922) as Ford perfected his mass production techniques.

Ford's refusal to diversify his product line led to a decline in the market share his company held against more creative competitors. By 1927, when Ford finally relented and discon-tinued the model, more than 15 million "Tin Lizzies" had been sold. Those millions of cars gave Americans free-dom and mobility that was the envy of the world and changed the nation profoundly over the years.

Henry Ford's moving assembly line, Highland Park, Michigan, circa 1913

Below, tire manufacturing at Goodyear Tire & Rubber Co. in Akron, Ohio, 1908; right, inventor Charles F. Kettering; below right, hand-cranking a 1910 Buick before Kettering's invention

A Booming Industry Makes Driving Safe and Comfortable

The auto industry soon became a powerful force in the American economy. Innovators and entrepreneurs turned out a steady stream of products that made cars safer, more reliable and more comfortable. As sales of cars skyrocketed, new industries, employing hundreds of thousands of workers, arose to make the parts and accessories that were needed.

Old industries were rescued and revamped by the booming auto industry. Petroleum — which was finding itself obsolete in the era of electric lamps — found a new market. Gasoline, once an undesirable by-product of petroleum, was now in high demand. The breakup of Standard Oil, under the Sherman Antitrust Act in 1911, created 33 separate companies at the same moment that the popularity of the automobile was creating a new industry. (1911 was also the first year that gasoline sales topped kerosene sales.) The juxtaposition of these two events reorganized the oil industry, separating it into refining, producing, shipping and marketing areas. As marketing to the growing millions of automobile owners became more of a focus, many oil companies opened "filling" stations across the country.

One early inventor and entrepreneur in auto-related industries was Charles F. Kettering. The founder of Dayton Engineering Laboratories Company (later shortened to Delco), he was also responsible for numerous performance-enhancing inventions. In 1912, Kettering developed an electrical system, including an electric "self-starter," that eliminated the need for hand-cranking, thus making it easier and safer for men and women to enjoy the pleasure and convenience of driving. Kettering also had a hand in creating leaded gasolines.

The need for automobile tires stimulated the growth of companies like Firestone Tire & Rubber — the supplier of tires for Ford's Model T — and Goodyear Tire & Rubber Co., which was transformed from a bicycle tire manufacturer into one of the first suppliers of automobile tires in 1899. Still a burgeoning industry, automobile tires for gas, steam and electric cars were made almost entirely by hand.

In 1904, Goodyear marketed the first tire with a detachable rim, which helped simplify the task — all too frequent in the age of unpaved roads — of changing flat tires. By 1917 Goodyear had become the largest tire manufacturer in the world.

The success of the auto industry lies in automotive engineering and the innovations of these supporting industries, which have made automobile travel safer, more pleasant and accessible to almost everyone.

The Wright Brothers Usher in a New Age

Though most newspapers missed the story, the age of flight began on the beach at Kitty Hawk, North Carolina, in 1903, with the brief flights of the Wright brothers' *Flyer 1*. Others before them had successfully flown gliders and unmanned craft, such as Samuel Langley's steam-powered airplane, but theirs was the first successful powered, manned flight.

With the experimentation of so many great men having gone before them, the public and the press initially

Above, the Wright Brothers' first flight at Kitty Hawk, December 7, 1903; below, Boeing's B & W Model 1, circa 1916

gave no validity to the Wright brothers' achievement; however, it was precisely this anonymity which allowed the brothers to develop the first airplane. As they worked, they followed only what principles they could prove for themselves (or could observe in the flight of natural aviators — birds) and often strayed far from popular ideas about manned flight. Langley and other heavily funded pioneers concentrated on using powerful engines. The Wright brothers, working with no outside funding, realized aeronautical stability was the key. Once they perfected gliding, adding an engine was relatively simple.

The Wright brothers' major innovation lay in devising a control system of rudders that allowed the pilot to twist the wing tips — based on the flight of buzzards — to preserve the plane's balance. In the following years, the Wrights and other aviation pioneers steadily expanded the possibilities of flight, stimulating the growth of an industry that would eventually become vital to defense, commerce and leisure travel.

The first warplanes saw action in World War I; even seaplanes were employed, not too successfully, in an effort to combat the German zeppelins. Death-defying air mail and primitive passenger services were launched, and the exploits of barnstormers and trick flyers stopped hearts all over the country. Many of the early stunts were proving grounds for new instruments and designs, and some of America's foremost aerospace companies were born in these early days. William E. Boeing, for instance, flew his first plane, the B&W Model 1, in 1916 and formed what is now The Boeing Company the same year.

Left, interior of Alcoa's first plant in Pittsburgh, Pennsylvania; below, aluminum pioneer Charles Martin Hall as a young man

Aluminum Helps Put Planes in the Air

The most abundant metal in the earth's crust, aluminum was once considered a precious metal like silver. Aluminum is found in nature chemically combined with other elements and wasn't extracted until the early 1800s, but it was so expensive to produce that it had few practical uses. Thus this material, now more closely associated with the ubiquitous soda can than the jewelry and carvings that the first pure aluminum was molded into, bloomed into the third most valuable manufacturing metal rather late.

In the 1880s, Charles Martin Hall and Paul-Louis-Toussaint Héroult independently developed an electrical extraction process just as abundant, cheap electricity was becoming available. One of the first industries to move into the Niagara Falls area after the first large hydroelectric plant went into operation there was the Pittsburgh Reduction Company, founded by Hall, which became the Aluminum Company of America (Alcoa) in 1907. Spurred by cheap power, the development of new alloys that strengthened aluminum and new markets for the metal, Alcoa alone was producing 16,500 short tons a year by 1909, up from 50 pounds a day in 1888. But the popularization of aluminum did not happen overnight; experimental products, including aluminum horse shoes and pots and pans (costing six times as much as the alternative tin pans) could not convince people of the utility of this new material. Aluminum was nice — but it wasn't necessary.

The first application for which aluminum was widely used was electrical equipment, since it combined light weight, high conductivity and malleability. Still, aluminum did not have the glamorous appeal of steel — that is, until the Wright brothers went looking for a way to lift man up into the sky. Aluminum was essential to the aircraft industry right from the start: the plane flown by the Wright brothers at Kitty Hawk, North Carolina, in 1903 was powered by an engine with an aluminum crankcase. Due to its relatively light weight, aluminum was used as a sheathing material on almost all airplanes. Its unique combination of properties was finally phenomenally demonstrated.

Aluminum production soared during World War I due to its use for war materials; it continued to rise after the war as new alloys and applications were discovered. Today, aluminum is exceeded only by iron and steel as a frequently used metal.

A New Material With A Million Uses

In Yonkers, New York, in 1907, Leo Baekeland stared at the result of his failed experiment to produce synthetic shellac in his backyard laboratory. His error had produced a hard, clear solid that would usher in a new world of man-made materials — a plastic that was impervious to acids, heat and electricity. The new material, called Bakelite, would have myriad uses touching Americans' lives in myriad ways: airplane parts, radio cabinets, buttons, toilet seats, machine parts, insulators, billiard balls and telephones, to name a few.

Bakelite introduced the age of plastics: cheap, moldable materials with seemingly endless uses. Today, U.S. production of plastic surpasses even that of steel and includes specialized materials created to meet particular challenges, from stopping bullets to pumping blood through the human body. Further, the value of this versatile, non-depletable resource has grown, following intense efforts to make recycling of this reusable material simple and convenient. Plastics are now omnipresent, with applications ranging from spacecraft and computers to golf clubs and bicycles.

An Engineering Triumph Serves Trade and Defense

Visionaries had dreamed of a canal across Central America since Balboa's first view of the Pacific in 1513. By the turn of the century, Americans had compelling reasons to shorten the long ocean voyage from its eastern to its western coast, which required rounding often-stormy Cape Horn. The United States had become an active world power with colonies and trading interests on both sides of the globe, and a canal would serve both national defense and commerce. The NAM, recognizing such benefits, was an early and active promoter of the project.

The Panama Canal, which took about 10 years and $380 million to build, is one of the world's greatest feats of engineering. Where the French had failed to engineer the task, the United States met the major construction challenges: massive amounts of earth that had to be excavated, mammoth locks that raise and lower ships during transit and gates that close the locks. American manufacturers supplied huge steam shovels, pile drivers and dredges, along with boats and locomotives, to clear out 239 million cubic yards of earth (the equivalent of 70 Great Pyramids). The gates, some of them weighing over 700 tons, were constructed of steel plates attached to a skeleton of steel girders and moved on hinges. Successfully meeting the challenges they posed represented a triumph of metalworking and the mastery of steel as a construction and manufacturing material. From Eberhard Faber Co.'s pencils and Hart, Schafner & Marx clothing, to Ingersoll-Rand's drills and Bethlehem Steel Company's steel supplies, American manufacturers provided every necessary item for the ten year project.

Essentially completed in 1914, the Panama Canal has been a vital link between the oceans for the United States, promoting the growth of the country's economic might, as well as its national security. In its first full year of operation, about 5 million tons of cargo were shipped through the canal; today the yearly average is about 140 million tons of raw materials and manufactured goods. Approximately 32 ships a day utilize the canal, each paying an average of $28,000 and displacing about 52 million gallons of water into the ocean from the man-made Gatun Lake which supplies the locks.

Top left, inventor Leo Baekeland; left, Bakelite pendant; opposite, the battleship *Ohio* passes through the Culebra Cut of the brand new Panama Canal, 1915

Left, inventor Lee De Forest holding the audio and oscillating tube; below, Reginald Fessenden, July 19, 1923

A Small Tube Paves the Way for the Radio Age

The triode vacuum tube patented by Dr. Lee De Forest in 1907 provided the missing link that made the Radio Age possible. Guglielmo Marconi had successfully transmitted signals with wireless equipment in the 1890s, and Reginald A. Fessenden had first broadcast the human voice on Christmas Eve 1906 to an audience of wireless operators on ships in the Atlantic. Wide-scale broadcasting of the human voice, however, required a means of amplification yet to be developed. The missing piece was provided when Lee De Forest placed a zigzag wire between two electrodes in a vacuum tube to produce the first tri-ode vacuum tube, which effectively amplified weak electronic signals.

Until the early 1920s, most people thought the main purpose of radio would be transatlantic and marine communication. De Forest didn't pursue the commercial possibilities of his invention for many years, and it was World War I that eventually provided the driving impetus for its use. The U.S. government used its war powers to suspend patent rights during the war and, seeing the promise of radio for battlefield communication, built thousands of radios and trained soldiers in their use. After the war, the skills these military broadcasters brought home with them helped to stimulate the fledgling radio industry, the development of which took most by surprise.

Most of the devices which bring the outside world into the home and into people's everyday lives have developed from this early technology. De Forest's vacuum tube, refined over the years, was crucial not only for the development of radio, but for telephones, radar, television and computers, as well. Until the invention of the transistor, the triode vacuum tube was an integral part of all such equipment.

Carrier Improves on Nature's Air

In 1902, on a foggy night in Pittsburgh, Willis Haviland Carrier lit upon the idea that enables the United States to keep cool. Two of the three crucial components of air conditioning — refrigeration and electricity — were familiar to engineers, but it was Carrier who made its commercialization possible by, among other technical breakthroughs, working out the third component, the means to dehumidify air. Mother Nature had supplied the crucial missing link, condensation, but Carrier is credited with designing the first scientific system to control the cleanliness, temperature and humidity of air.

The demands of industry and the need to combat oppressive heat prompted the installation of the first air conditioner in 1903. Carrier's invention cooled the Sackett-Wilhelms Lithographing and Publishing Company building, a task that would have required 108,000 pounds of ice, while keeping the humidity at 55 percent. Cooler, drier conditions were critical for many industries, and Carrier crossed America installing climate-control systems in factories, plants and mills.

Productivity and efficiency quickly increased in air-conditioned factories. Air conditioning in trains, apartments, homes and public buildings followed after 1925, when the Rivoli Theatre in New York City made the move to air conditioning. Until then, theaters brought in large blocks of ice and ran fans to circulate the cool wet air. But at the debut performance of Carrier's system in 1925, the air conditioning stopped the skeptical, fanning moviegoers "cold." The increase in box office sales that summer alone ($100,000) was more than enough to pay for the installation of the air-conditioning unit. Theater executives were thrilled at the prospect of elimi-

nating the typical summer slump, and numerous theaters leapt at this opportunity to boost their sales. Many a moviegoer in those days appreciated the cool air inside the theater just as much as the movie — and wondered about using a similar system inside his or her own home, office or factory.

The resulting popularity of air conditioning kept the Carrier Air Conditioning Company of America strong through the Great Depression and changed forever the home and workplace. It also played a significant role in the rapid growth and development of cities such as Houston and Las Vegas. The air conditioner has brought increased comfort, better health and higher productivity through a temperature-controlled environment.

Above, J.L. Hudson's, the first air-conditioned department store, Detroit, Michigan, 1924; below, the Rivoli Theatre, Times Square, New York City, 1925

Living Gets Easier with Electrical Appliances

Perhaps nothing better exemplifies the tremendous impact manufacturing has had on America than home appliances. The first two decades of the twentieth century brought a host of new electrical appliances that would help to transform household life and labor. Electric washing machines first appeared in 1910, and once Maytag developed a successful casting process for an aluminum-tub model in 1919, sales of electric washers catapulted. General Electric brought out the first electric toaster in 1912; Black and Decker initiated the sale of electric hand drills in 1917. The electric vacuum cleaner was patented in 1908 by Murray Spengler, who joined forces with his cousin, William B. Hoover, to found the Hoover Company.

Such inventions — continually being improved upon — began a process that has marked the twentieth century: the easing of the burden of work. The toaster, for instance, was modified further by McGraw Electric Company in the twenties to "pop" the slices out of the vertical toasting slots on schedule with an internal timer. By eliminating the need for waiting and turning the toast, a simple but time-consuming task could be performed even more easily. Looking back today, it is hard to imagine how anyone had the time to take care of all the daily workings of the home. The time and energy that these and other machines saved people changed American home life beyond recognition, leading to major changes in the lifestyles of the people who did most domestic tasks — women.

Above, *The Home Electrical*, by an unknown artist, 1912; opposite, electric vacuum cleaner, circa 1910

Industry Meets Wartime Challenge and Change

The ingenuity, dedication, efficient assembly lines and overtime work of American manufacturers enabled the United States' factories to produce the matériel to help defeat its enemies in World War I. With only 55 airplanes and 208,034 men in the army when the war began, industry had to make up the difference between an army without enough blankets for its new recruits and the formidable force that won a decisive victory with 116,516 casualties.

During the war, America exported huge amounts of chemicals, steel, munitions and food, and the balance of trade shifted decisively, with exports exceeding imports by $3.6 billion in 1917. By war's end, factories were turning out great amounts of both traditional and new weapons,

including 875 ships and 15,000 V-12 Liberty engines, which standardized Allied aircraft and went from the drawing board to full production in only a few months. About 300,000 trucks were built for the armed forces in 1917 alone.

No wartime change in America had a greater effect on American manufacturers than did the proliferation of government agencies — more than 500 in number — such as the War Industries Board, Food Administration, Fuel Administration, War Labor Board and Shipping Board, which rationed natural resources and set industry's priorities. No wartime change had a greater effect on the American labor force than did the "drafting" of women into factories, mills, offices, mechanics' shops —

nearly every area of work — to replace the doughboys overseas. Many an image of women riveting aluminum plane panels on a World War II assembly line comes to mind, but that famous image was born in World War I, when women got their foot in the door of American industry.

America's achievements in World War I placed the mantle of world leadership on the nation's brawny shoulders — a mantle that the country was not yet fully ready to wear. Though the country's focus turned to domestic affairs during the decade that followed, the mighty industrial machine that had gained vigor from wartime production was kept well tuned by providing consumer goods that would further enhance America's ever-rising standards of living.

Bas-relief of oil field workers photographed by Michael Puig; opposite page, Charles A. Lindbergh moments before his solo flight, 1927

CHAPTER THREE

Business Booms During the Jazz Age

1 9 2 0 - 1 9 2 9

It was the greatest, gaudiest spree in history," so F. Scott Fitzgerald described the 1920s. It was the age of Prohibition and speakeasies, of the Charleston and the flapper. It was the age of the automobile, which affected people's mobility and mindset. It was the age of incredible feats, like the first solo nonstop airplane flight across the Atlantic, and the age of unbelievably silly stunts, such as sitting atop a flagpole for days. It was the age of great heroes — "Lucky Lindy" and "the Babe" — as well as notorious criminals like Al Capone. It was, in short, an age filled with exuberant people and exuberant events — exuberance itself.

The twenties also represented a period of hitherto unparalleled economic growth. Between 1919 and 1929, both the nation's GNP and per capita income increased prodigiously. At the same time, the average workweek in manufacturing declined by 10 percent. Companies began looking beyond efficiency, viewing employees as valued "human resources." By 1925, nearly 500 companies, half in manufacturing, were publishing employee magazines. Automobile production more than trebled, and by 1927, more than one out of every two American families had a car. For families in most parts of the country, this meant more possible locations for employment and more opportunity to see the U.S.A.

Certain other industries helped pave the way for this largely prosperous decade; radio sales, for instance, skyrocketed from $2 million to $600 million. The chemical, telephone and movie industries forged ahead, as did the building industry and chain stores — led by F. W. Woolworth; Sears, Roebuck and Co.; J. C. Penney; and the Great Atlantic and Pacific Tea Co. (today's A&P) — proof of the growing and prospering American population, which now enjoyed increased leisure time and a wider variety of affordable manufactured goods. Electrical utilities also helped to power the economic growth.

Similarly, foreign commerce contributed to the boom, despite the enactment of tariffs to protect the domestic market and resultant difficulties encountered with trade partners. The National Association of Manufacturers during this time redirected its efforts from promotional activities on behalf of individual companies to those which more broadly advanced global commerce. Many agreed with President Calvin Coolidge's simple pronouncement that "the business of America is business."

Some apparently believed that good times were permanent, that up-and-down economic cycles were part of the past. In retrospect, serious problems loomed below the surface. Nonetheless, lavish investment catapulted the stock market to dizzying heights. The skeptical economist Roger Babson warned that "sooner or later a crash is coming, and it may be terrific."

On October 29, 1929, "Black Friday," the market plunged into a free fall. Within a month, stocks had lost 40 percent of their value, or $30 billion. The Jazz Age was about to give way to the Depression Decade.

The Auto Age Creates New Opportunities

The automobile market was changing in significant ways during the twenties. Ford's Model T, the market leader for years, never changed, but some of Ford's competitors began to cut into its sales by offering new styles and services to customers. General Motors, under the leadership of Alfred P. Sloan (who became its CEO in 1923), produced a wide range of cars at different price levels and invested heavily in advertising to attract consumers. As a result, from 1920 to 1926, GM's share of the market grew from 20 to 30 percent, overtaking Ford. The Chrysler Corporation followed a similar strategy and, by the late 1920s, had become one of the three biggest automakers. After having produced 15 million "Tin Lizzies," Ford bowed to market trends and brought out a new model, the Model A, in 1928.

The automobile had profound cultural effects. It made suburbanization possible, exposed rural dwellers to the cities (and vice versa) and offered an unprecedented degree of mobility that increased possible work and leisure destinations.

Numerous businesses sprang up to serve the consumer and safety needs of these mobile Americans. Wintry driving conditions called for large quantities of rock salt and other products. Traffic lights, which had first appeared in Cleveland, Ohio, in 1914, helped control the traffic on increasingly congested city streets. The introduction of laminated safety glass, such as PPG Industries' Duplate in 1928, ensured that auto glass would become a booming part of the glass industry.

Hertz began its car rental business with a dozen Model T Fords in 1918, and by the 1920s, rental car companies were competing furiously for the business of out-of-towners who determined that they could no longer "get around" without the help of an automobile. Roadside motels and filling stations multiplied to accommodate business travelers and vacationing families. Manufacturers' sales representatives benefited from this increased mobility.

Following the first Indianapolis 500 in 1911, the racing of cars grew in popularity and gave manufacturers a chance to advertise their newly designed products as sponsors of various racing teams. Soon many typical activities were tailored to the needs (and whims) of drivers. The first drive-in movie theater would appear in 1933 in Camden, New Jersey. The first Marriott A&W Root Beer stand appeared in 1927 on 14th Street in the nation's capital.

Whether it was a Ford, Chevrolet, Chrysler or car from a host of other manufacturers, the automobile was at the center of the major trends of the 1920s. It was both cause and effect of the decade's growth and prosperity. The public's demand for cars stimulated rapid growth in many sectors of manufacturing — including steel, plate glass, petroleum and rubber. It has been estimated that by 1929, the jobs of one in four American workers already depended on the automobile directly or indirectly.

Opposite, a Sunoco service station, 1930s; above, Chrysler Corporation, Highland Park, Michigan, circa 1929

Communicating Across Town, Across Country, Across Oceans

As the world becomes a "global community" of many nations, no one factor is more important in the breaking down of the barriers of distance than long-distance communication. Ease of communication allows manufacturers and multinational corporations to pursue business opportunities at farther reaches of the globe with efficiency. Today, it's as easy to talk to a friend or business associate overseas as it is to talk to a neighbor.

Long-distance voice communications began with the telephone, invented by Alexander Graham Bell in 1876 and enhanced by various improvements over the years, including the vacuum-tube amplifier.

Members of President Woodrow Wilson's cabinet advocated, unsuccessfully, placing ownership of the telephone system within the postal service. By 1915, when the network of phone lines made transcontinental phone calls possible, nearly every home and office was equipped to take advantage of this network. However, where the land stopped, so did the phone lines. There was still no way to communicate by voice over the ocean.

A breakthrough in this field occurred on January 14, 1923, when two American Telephone and Telegraph Company officials — one in the company's New York headquarters, the other in its London office — conversed. Their two-hour talk marked the first transatlantic telephone call, which was transmitted through the air via short-wave radio.

Though the radio had been in existence for several years already, the use of a special 20-valve loudspeaker greatly improved both the strength and the fidelity of transoceanic exchange and paved the way for further improvements in the field. Within a decade, radio-transmitted overseas telephone calls, while not yet commonplace, were

facilitating global communications. Certainly telephones had the effect of diminishing the limits of time and space, enabling a more rapid flow of information between individuals separated by thousands of miles of ocean.

In 1956, the same company, AT&T, took the development of transoceanic communication one step further when it completed the laying of the first transatlantic telephone cables — 90 years after the completion of the first transatlantic telegraph cable. The

technology for laying undersea cables had been available for many years, but successful audio communication over such a distance depended on amplifiers (called repeaters) to counteract signal loss over distance. The undersea cable became practical when technology provided repeaters with a 20-year life span. On the first day of commercial service, the cable carried 75 percent more service than a typical day of radio calls, confirming the judgment of those at AT&T who called it "the perfect product."

Above, transatlantic cable being pulled ashore, Clarenville, New Jersey, 1956; below, telephone operators handling international calls, 1929

Radio Breaks New Ground in Entertainment and Advertising

While most of the major advances of this century came about when technology caught up with a particular need, there have been historical moments, such as the advent of commercial radio, when existing technology filled a need people didn't know they had.

Amateur and experimental radio stations proliferated after World War I, but the commercial possibilities had not yet been perceived. KDKA in Pittsburgh is usually considered the birthplace of professional broadcasting (though WWJ in Detroit vies for that status). KDKA grew from an experimental station run by Frank Conrad, a Westinghouse employee and radio enthusiast, who began broadcasting records over the air for the pleasure of a few amateur radio operators who could receive his signal.

Soon the local music store offered Conrad free records if he would mention the store during his broadcasts. Then a local department store started selling radio receivers that could pick up this "free" music — for only $10. Westinghouse soon recognized the commercial possibilities of combining broadcasting with radio sales: the more there was to listen to, the more people would want to buy radios. The company obtained a broadcasting license for a station with the call letters KDKA and went on the air in time to broadcast the 1920 presidential election returns.

Radio production and broadcasting grew spectacularly during the decade. By 1924, there were 500 licensed radio stations around the country. The earliest radios were large consoles designed to look like a piece of furniture, around which the family could quite literally gather. With

Station KDKA, as Harding-Cox election returns are broadcast, 1920

companies like RCA producing radios by the thousands, radio ownership leapt from 0.2 percent of American homes in 1922 to 60 percent in 1932. The new medium connected Americans in an entirely new way: people could hear the same news at almost the same time, swoon over the same singers' voices and share the excitement of a home run in Yankee Stadium. Radios transmitted news, sports events, entertainment and advertising.

Their wide distribution did more than initiate a common, or popular, culture — it determined what that culture was. As the consumer economy was developing, radios prodded that economic trend along: businesses learned to use radio advertising to broadcast the glories of their products and services. This development of commercial communication for entertainment and advertising purposes paved the way for the lightning-swift rise of television decades later. It would not be long before radio networks that sprang up, beginning with the National Broadcasting Company in 1926 and the Columbia Broadcasting System in 1929, would have the technology to bring not just sound, but a picture, into American homes.

A drink to the health of the Family

Fresh Food and Fewer Shopping Trips

In the early decades of the twentieth century, home refrigeration was provided by iceboxes, with the ice man arriving several times a week to deliver the blocks of ice needed to chill the food. Mechanical refrigeration units which ran on gas or other natural fuel were bulky, costly and in need of constant supervision. They had been used only by ice and meatpacking firms and for some specialized warehousing.

Kelvinator had developed an electrical refrigeration unit in 1916, but it was the development of the fractional horsepower electric motor in the 1920s that enabled the smaller size and greater efficiency of the electric refrigerator.

The widely selling Leonard "refrigerator cabinet" was actually an icebox specially designed with the option of using Kelvinator's electric cooling device, instead of ice, to keep food fresh if the customer so wished. However, the cooling device was still so cumbersome that it was usually installed in the basement. Kelvinator was so early onto the scene of home electric refrigerators that of the 10,000 units in use in 1922, more than three quarters were Kelvinators.

The first electric refrigerator to incorporate the refrigeration device directly in the icebox, introduced in 1925 by Kelvinator, opened up the market drastically and was copied by several refrigerator manufacturers, including Frigidaire, Westinghouse, General Electric and Hotpoint. Kelvinator's 93,000 units represented only 12 percent of the electric refrigerators in use by 1929. That year Frigidaire, another industry leader, took the obvious next step, introducing the first chest-type freezer for the home. Since then, American households have become dependent on electrical refrigeration for fresh, safe food and fewer shopping trips than had previously been necessary.

In time, U.S. manufacturers would respond to the needs of an increasingly affluent society by producing refrigerators and freezers in a variety of sizes, styles and colors. By reducing the demands of housekeeping, such appliances allowed homemakers to turn their attention and energy elsewhere.

Advertisement for Frigidaire's electric refrigerator

The 'Talkies Entertain, Enchant and Enliven

For many living in the small towns springing up across the country in the 1920s, what was known of good times in the big city and romance in far-off lands was learned from the silver screen. It was the golden age of motion pictures, and by the end of the decade, the average weekly attendance for the nation's movie theaters numbered approximately 100 million.

Behind this boom were enormous technological advances in the movies as well as photography in general. Technicolor, Inc. invented the process which bears its name and which was used in several films of the decade — notably *The Black Pirate*, which opened in 1926 and starred the swashbuckling Douglas Fairbanks. The first motion picture with sound, *Don Juan*, was released the same year, although the success of the costly "talkies" was assured only the following year with the appearance of *The Jazz Singer*, with Al Jolson.

By using a microphone developed by Lee De Forest, which recorded sounds as different intensities of electric current and "played" the current through a light bulb, filmmakers could film two tracks at once — one for the picture, one for the sound.

Though, like most Kodak products, the Kodacolor film introduced in 1928 was designed to put better equipment in the hands of amateurs, the new film made its appearance in big-time studios as well. The same year witnessed another triumph of technological virtuosity: the first all-color, all-sound musical motion picture, *On with the Show.*

Along with the radio, movies brought a new type of popular culture to America, with people all over the country humming the same songs, dancing the same dances, thrilling to the same stories. The movie industry had already relocated from the East Coast to Hollywood and was completing the process of organizing itself into a few powerful Hollywood studios. The "star system" also characterized the decade, bringing to the silver screen such moviegoer favorites as Charlie Chaplin, Stan Laurel and Oliver Hardy, the Gish sisters, Rudolph Valentino, Douglas Fairbanks, Mary Pickford, Greta Garbo and Gloria Swanson.

In future years, television — predicted by the first transatlantic transmission of photographs (from England to the United States) in 1924 — and television personalities would further develop this mass culture.

Left, movie poster, 1931; above, famed explorer Martin Johnson with two of the first all-metal Bell & Howell Company professional movie cameras

Aviation Pioneers Popularize Air Travel

As aviators tested the limits of flight, Americans viewed them as pioneers and cheered their efforts to fly ever farther and faster. One of history's most celebrated flights was the solo Atlantic crossing completed by Charles A. Lindbergh in 1927. Lindbergh flew a specially designed Ryan M-2 monoplane with a Wright-built engine. The best-known aircraft in aviation history — the *Spirit of St. Louis* — featured numerous advances, including the world's first flared tube fitting introduced by Parker Hannifin Corporation and still standard in aircraft today.

Jimmy Doolittle, a World War I aviator who became a lieutenant general in World War II, crossed another aviation threshold on September 24, 1929, when he piloted a plane with a hood that cut off his view of the world outside his cockpit. With no visual clues available, he had to rely on instruments alone to take off, circle the airfield and land.

Still another pilot laid claim to a place in the skies for women. Amelia Earhart flew her Lockheed Vega solo across the Atlantic in 1928 — the first woman to do so — then made the first successful solo flight from Hawaii to California in 1935.

The pioneers of flight were not always pushing just the limits of distance and endurance. The annual air races in Cleveland, Ohio — sponsored by manufacturing leaders, including former NAM President Frederick Crawford of Thompson Products (now TRW) — featured fearless pilots who also pushed the limits of speed.

Lindbergh, Doolittle, Earhart and other flyers were idolized by the public. As they tamed the perils of flight, they also helped Americans get used to the idea that humans could safely soar above the clouds. Before long, many of the people who followed radio broadcasts tracking those early flights would themselves be boarding passenger planes manufactured by Boeing, Douglas, Convair, Lockheed and others.

Standing behind these aviation pioneers were other kinds of heroes — inventors like Elmer Sperry, whose work took much of the danger out of flying. After pursuing ventures in electricity and coal mining technology, Sperry had turned his energies to the development of improved ship gyroscopes and a practical gyrocompass that would help steel-hulled ships and submarines preserve a steady course. He established the Sperry Gyroscope Company in 1910, and in 1911, the first gyrocompass was installed on the Battleship *Delaware*. Within a few years, it was standard equipment on navy ships and coming into common use by steamship lines.

The airplane industry was waiting for a development just like Sperry's. Gyroscopic instruments solved a major aviation problem: pilots had a false sense of direction when they couldn't see the horizon, so bad weather and poor visibility were always extremely dangerous. Though Sperry's invention could save lives, pilots were reluctant to rely on instruments after years of flying by sight. However, Charles Lindbergh had come to trust the gyroscopic turn indicator while flying as a mail pilot in 1926, learning that it was more reliable than his senses. This same confidence in his instruments enabled him the following year to pull out of two spins over the Atlantic and make it all the way to Paris.

By developing a flight control system based on gyroscopes, Sperry helped move aviation from a hobby to a promising commercial enterprise and enable pilots to do what even birds could not — fly blind. He went on to develop increasingly sophisticated instruments, culminating in the first successful automatic pilot in 1930. Today, gyroscopes enhance the precision of weapons and missiles, and steady spacecraft on their long journeys.

Above, Sperry Gyroscope engineer's department, World War I; right, Elmer Sperry and the gyropilot, circa 1923

Opposite, Charles A. Lindbergh shortly before his solo flight across the Atlantic, 1927

Right, Professor Robert H. Goddard, 1924; below, Goddard with the first rocket he experimented with

On the blackboard:
limit of balloon: 20 miles — Moon
limit of atmosphere: 200 miles
EARTH

Goddard Paves the Way for Space Exploration

At the age of 18, Robert H. Goddard found in rocketry a mission worthy of a lifetime of earnest pursuit. Though his place in history as the father of space exploration and the credit due him were bestowed posthumously, the limits of the path he opened for the world have yet to be reached.

A professor of physics at Clark University in Worcester, Massachusetts, Goddard had begun seriously experimenting with rockets during World War I. A decade later, in 1926, he launched the first rocket ever to employ liquid fuel, in this instance,

liquid oxygen, which combined with gasoline placed in its two-foot-long motor. The rocket, which was 10 feet high, reached an altitude of 41 feet and a distance of 184 feet in its 2.5 seconds of firing. This modest flight prefigured the stunning marvels of rocketry that would become familiar later in the century.

Goddard went on to test other concepts that helped lead to the development of missiles, satellites and space exploration. Though he had the support of Charles Lindbergh, modest grants from the Smithsonian

Institution and more substantial support from the Daniel and Florence Guggenheim Foundation, he never had sufficient funding to test his design for a rocket that could escape from the earth's gravitational pull. By the middle of World War II, his work had been outpaced by German rocket designers, though their early rockets were similar to his designs and may well have borrowed from his patents.

Though space travel is still an experimental field, Goddard's ideas and research have changed our world in ways that are still unfolding.

Modern communication satellites, space flights and lunar landings owe much to his path-breaking efforts. For instance, the upper stages of the *Saturn V* that carried American astronauts to the moon were powered by the same fuel and oxidizer Goddard used in many of his rockets. His ultimate vision — vehicles that would enable humans to settle on other planets — may yet become reality.

PVC Makes a New World of Products Possible

While plastics continue their evolution today as materials of a thousand uses, very few plastics are household names. "Polyvinyl chloride" may not ring a bell for everybody, but most manufacturers and many consumers know that any product made with "PVC," today the second most widely used plastic, is going to do the job — and keep doing it for a long time.

In 1926, Dr. Waldo Semon, an employee of B.F. Goodrich, accidentally discovered a method for producing PVC while trying to develop an adhesive with special properties. The material he came up with didn't have the characteristics he sought, but it did have other unique and useful properties. At first limited to such industrial applications as coating wires and cables, PVC's great strength, flexibility and resistance to chemicals helped it become a staple in the manufacture of consumer goods after World War II. In such diverse items as drainage pipe, raincoats, upholstery fabrics, floor coverings, shower curtains, films and phonograph records — as well as the ubiquitous credit card — PVC revolutionized old products and allowed the creation of new ones that we take for granted today.

Above, laying PVC pipe; right, Dr. Waldo Semon (in shirtsleeves) at work

Mechanization Makes Farm Production Soar

The tractor transformed farming and helped make the U.S. the world's premier agricultural nation, but it first proved its utility not in a farm field, but on the battlefield. Aware of early tractors' shortcomings, farmers were reluctant to make the change from horse-drawn equipment. "Tractors" had been available since the 1870s, but few farmers purchased the huge, four-wheeled, steam-driven contraptions. They produced plenty of power to run harvesting equipment, but they were too awkward to till fields.

Tractors with internal gasoline engines hit the scene in the early 1900s. The predecessors of modern tractors,

they were small and easy to drive but were limited in capability by their less powerful engines. Even following Benjamin Holt's invention of the familiar track-type Caterpillar tractor, the farming industry was slow to convert. By 1910, there were only about 1,000 tractors on American farms.

Holt's design did not go unnoticed by the military, however. Inspired by a muddy river delta near San Francisco, Caterpillars held up in the toughest, muckiest conditions of World War I, hauling cannons to the front. Full-fledged military tanks were later developed from Holt's track design. Following the war, the sale of track-type tractors took off, and agriculture took on an increasingly mechanized character as draft horses were displaced by the more efficient and durable machines. General-purpose tractors became powerful enough for plowing, but tall and light enough for cultivating.

The recession after World War I was tough on the farm equipment sector, starting an industrywide shakeout. Of 157 such manufacturers in 1917, there were only 18 in 1929. Nonetheless, such successful manufacturers as Caterpillar, J. I. Case, John Deere, International Harvester, Allis Chalmers and others introduced further product refinements in the 1930s and beyond, contributing substantially to the amazing productivity of American agriculture at mid-century, as well as to the growing size of farms.

Opposite top, a Case Model W Hillside Combine, in Colton, Washington, 1929; opposite bottom, one of Benjamin Holt's early track-type crawlers being tested on grounds adjacent to plant; this page, above an artist's impression of a tractor pull between Case and John Deere tractors; above left, Old Abe, Case Corporation's logo since 1884

Detail of *Construction of the Dam* by William Gropper; opposite page, molten metal pours during production of steel

CHAPTER FOUR

The Great Depression Tests Ingenuity

1 9 3 0 - 1 9 4 0

Seeking to buoy public confidence, President Herbert Hoover announced in December 1929 that "conditions are fundamentally sound." For a similar reason, John D. Rockefeller disclosed that he had been buying stocks. (Joked comedian Eddie Cantor: "Sure, who else had any money left?") But neither the nation's chief executive nor its richest citizen could reverse the plunge into economic disaster. By the middle of 1932, the Great Depression had reached its nadir and showed no signs of abating. The value of stocks had decreased another $45 billion; industrial and agricultural prices had plunged to mind-boggling depths, and approximately 25 percent of the work force was unemployed. Not surprisingly, Hoover lost the 1932 presidential election to Franklin D. Roosevelt, who had promised a "new deal."

The New Deal was not a single coherent program. Rather, it was a series of experiments designed to produce immediate relief combined with long-term reforms. Overall, the government intervened more regularly, more willingly and more deeply than in any previous peacetime. This intervention profoundly alienated much of the business community. While the president emphasized that he was trying to save capitalism, many of his critics thought otherwise, and the economy was slow to revive.

Despite adverse times, the manufacturers who survived, large and small alike, adapted as they could and slowly began to recover. While fully one-half of all American industries did decline in absolute terms, chemical, electrical equipment and petroleum counted themselves growth industries during this decade. Inventions and innovative processes brought dramatic changes to the machine tool industry, and a variety of new consumer products emerged. The decade witnessed a number of remarkable "firsts": the jet engine, helicopter, electric typewriter, Kodachrome film, particle accelerator, fiberglass, nylon and the electro-mechanical analog computer, to name some. Additionally, the thirties witnessed the completion of such structural marvels as the Empire State Building, the Golden Gate Bridge and Boulder (later Hoover) Dam. Despite — but also because of — deeply troubled economic conditions, ingenuity had thrived, and the manufacturing community accomplished much.

As the thirties waned, the labor movement took advantage of changing public opinion. With a renewed interest in protecting their jobs, mass-production workers, largely ignored by the American Federation of Labor in the 1920s, formed the Congress of Industrial Organizations in 1938. The creation of this new union organization, and the inclusion of industrial workers in what had before been a labor movement focused on traditional craft unions, bolstered organized labor nationwide. Union membership rose from around 12 percent in 1933 to 30 percent by the end of the 1930s and began to play an increasingly larger role in manufacturing operations and industrial legislation.

As the decade closed, however, the nation's attention increasingly turned to the war clouds gathering in Europe and Asia.

Nylon Creates a Sensation

Though hard times kept people's pockets and bank accounts nearly empty, the pipelines of industrial research were still bustling. Well aware by this time of the potential for new types of plastics, manufacturers worked to develop several valuable synthetic materials during the Great Depression. Of these, the one that created perhaps the biggest stir was nylon.

After 11 years and $27 million, in 1938 DuPont announced the discovery of nylon by Wallace H. Carothers. In researching polymers, the research team had focused their efforts on amides, the chemical proteins that occur in natural fibers. "Strong as steel, delicate as a spider's web, yet more elastic than any of the natural fibers," this artificial silk was a huge success when the company brought it to market.

Stockings made of nylon became available nationwide in 1940 and caused such a sensation that first-day sales of the product created mob scenes. This miracle fiber had an extremely complicated production process and offered many advantages over most natural materials. It was resilient, durable, impervious to oil and quick drying. Its desirability increased as all consumer nylon production was halted to provide tents, parachutes and tire cording for World War II.

Nylon paved the way for the synthetic fiber textiles industry, which today offers numerous synthetic fibers to choose from: Dacron, Fortrel, Antron, Lycra and more. The properties of these new materials, as well as many other plastics, made possible new uses and new products, offering an expanded array of tools for work and play.

Dr. Paul Morgan, DuPont Company, demonstrating process for making nylon, 1961

Above, nylon ad; right, nylon stocking sale after
World War II, San Francisco, California

The DC-3 Convinces Americans to Fly

Despite the Depression, advances in aviation continued to build the United States commercial airline industry. The Douglas DC-3, the most popular passenger plane developed before World War II, was made possible by several major engineering breakthroughs. Aerodynamic advances brought streamlined, faster airplanes; variable-pitch propellers added thrust and efficiency; the automatic pilot made long flights less tedious for pilots; improved instruments tamed some of the hazards of bad-weather flight; and cabins were pressurized for safety and comfort.

The DC-3, which began airline service in 1936, benefited from all of these advances. It carried 21 passengers (or just 14 in a Pullman-type sleeper version) at 195 miles per hour. More importantly, it was the first plane to fly efficiently on passenger revenue alone. In an era when passenger service played second fiddle to the financially secure business of airmail, the DC-3 enabled major airlines to change the nature of their business and meet the demand for economic air transportation. About 15,000 of the twin-engine transports (also known as "Gooney Birds") were built by American manufacturers both to accommodate the growing number of passengers and for military use. Many are still in the air today.

With its safety, speed and comfort, the DC-3 launched a new chapter in transportation. Commercial air travel, if not yet routine, was coming of age. The automobile opened up the continent to roving Americans; it wouldn't be long before the airplane would open up the world.

Above, Douglas DC-3; below, Douglas plant, Santa Monica, California, 1924

Burlington *Zephyr* train, 1934

Stainless Steel Stimulates New Designs

Built for the Chicago, Burlington and Quincy Railroad by the Edward G. Budd Manufacturing Company of Philadelphia, the *Zephyr*, powered by a diesel engine, made its first run in May 1934, traveling from Denver to Chicago in record time and setting a speed record of 112 miles per hour. The *Zephyr* was more than just a testament to the speed of the modern age; the cars' interior design incorporated the gamut of modern materials, including Formica tables and spun aluminum insulation. Most important was the design of the exterior shell; it was made of sleek, streamlined stainless steel in a spectacular art deco style.

Stainless steel, an alloy of steel and chromium, is notable for resisting corrosion and has been used in a wide variety of products, ranging from flatware and commercial kitchen equipment to parts for cars, airplanes, buildings and bridges. The combination of chromium and steel forms a coating of iron oxide and chromium that resists rust, bacteria, acid and soap. Seconds after a stainless steel surface is scratched, a new layer of the protective oxide forms.

Steel manufacturing was already one of the nation's most important industries, but in the 1930s stainless steel gave designers, architects and engineers a sensational new material that was both tough and beautiful. Its utility has made it the material of choice for innumerable products in the six decades since the *Zephyr*'s first trip, and the memory of the *Zephyr* lives on in the gleaming stainless steel diners across the country, which recall its art deco design.

Scotch Tape: A Humble Product Solves a Multitude of Needs

The world was waiting for Scotch tape — even if it didn't know it. The Minnesota Mining and Manufacturing Company, now known as 3M, developed and marketed the sticky cellophane tape that quickly became a fixture in homes and offices. From its early years, 3M had determined to make only products that filled a special need and therefore could command a premium price. Though they first concentrated on abrasives, the company went on to develop expertise in adhesives.

Thus, when car manufacturers needed a tape to delineate the color boundaries on two-tone auto bodies, 3M came up with masking tape in 1925. The tape could hold fast and was non-absorbent, yet could be removed without leaving a residue or removing the paint.

The solution was so perfect for the problem that when a St. Paul manufacturer needed a way to seal moisture-proof packages, it turned to 3M. In September 1930, the solution came — cellophane tape marketed under the Scotch brand. (The earliest masking tape had adhesive only on the edges, earning 3M a reputation as a thrifty — or "scotch" — company. 3M embraced the nickname, taking it on as a trademark.)

Thrifty families soon discovered that the tape was useful for mending items that they could not afford to replace, and the use of Scotch tape has continued to grow. Today, Scotch tape is found in 90 percent of homes doing everything from repairing torn photographs to splinting the broken bones of endangered birds.

More recently, 3M again introduced an answer to a common need when it marketed Post-it brand notes. Art Fry, the man who invented

Car painter using masking tape , circa 1920s

the product, worked in the company's adhesives division. When he found an adhesive seemingly too weak to hold securely, he used it to coat markers that would mark his place in his church choir hymnal without damaging the page when he removed it. From hymnals to cookbooks to presidential briefs, the Post-it note is now a fixture in many American workplaces and homes.

The Electric Typewriter Improves Office Efficiency

Thomas A. Edison first patented the electric typewriter in 1872, but it was IBM that marketed the first practical commercial model. The manufacturer of office machines, not yet 20 years old, had a vision for the electric typewriter. IBM purchased Northeast Electronic Company's model in 1933, redesigned it and offered the "Electromatic" to consumers one year later. The product's success stemmed from its ability to speed up the typing process, the ease and efficiency it offered typists and the uniform appearance of the key strokes.

In the years that followed, IBM introduced valuable innovations such as standardized spacing, the keypad-operated "carriage" return and the Selectric's ball-shaped typing mechanism, which offered interchangeable fonts and saved even the speediest of typists from jammed keys. More than the simple electrification of an old machine, it was IBM's refinement of its design and product quality that gave the electric typewriter its reputation and continually improved office efficiency over the decades that followed.

Sikorsky Brings da Vinci's Concept to Life

Helicopters added new dimensions to flight through their ability to hover, fly straight up and down, and make take-offs and landings in very small spaces. Such feats were not easy to achieve, however. From its original conception in the mind of Leonardo da Vinci to its first flight, the helicopter was 400 years in the making.

Russian-born aeronautical engineer Igor Sikorsky emigrated penniless to the United States immediately after the Russian Revolution. A pioneer in aviation —

he had designed and flown the world's first multi-motor plane in 1913 — he co-founded the Vought-Sikorsky Company in the 1920s to manufacture planes and flying boats. Entranced since his youth by da Vinci's vision of a prototypical helicopter, Sikorsky developed his own, the VS-300, in 1939 and first piloted it successfully the following year. His design solved a major aeronautical challenge posed by the single-rotor craft, which was the instability caused by the torque that the rotor's motion created.

Sikorsky's craft used a tail rotor to counteract this twisting force. In 1941, his helicopter set a world's record for helicopters by remaining aloft for more than an hour and a half.

While less than ideal for transportation of heavy payloads, helicopters quickly found practical uses for which airplanes were unsuitable, including military and rescue missions, crop-dusting, aerial observation, even construction, as well as meeting specialized transportation needs.

Birdseye's Process Brings Tasty Food to the Freezer

Even in the Depression's lean years, the Birds Eye brand of frozen foods offered such a welcome combination of good taste and convenience that the uniform little boxes became a standard item in American kitchens.

Numerous attempts at preserving food by freezing preceded Clarence Birdseye's invention of a successful process in 1924. Earlier efforts used ice, or ice and salt, but the slowness of the freezing process left foods damaged and unappetizing.

Birdseye had spent several years in Labrador as a fur trader and had noticed that fish caught on a day so cold that they froze almost immediately seemed to be tastier. Drawing on this observation, he developed a new process for freezing that incorporated an important innovation: the food was packaged prior to freezing, which allowed safe and sanitary contact with the freezing mechanism and a faster drop to the desired temperature. He used a rectangular package that could be easily placed between two chilled metal belts or plates, and the specially coated paper box protected the food from contact with equipment or chemicals.

Though his product excited curiosity, Birdseye was initially unable to market his frozen foods profitably. In 1929, his company, General Foods, was purchased by Postum, which subsequently adopted the name General Foods Corporation. However, the company had to contend with the limited demand for new products during the Great Depression. Development of a widespread market for frozen foods depended not only on improvements in home refrigerators (as well as the technology for shipping and displaying frozen foods), but also on intense marketing efforts by General Foods to change the popular conception of frozen foods as second rate, unfit for the dining room table and destined only for institutions.

The company worked with reluctant retailers to help promote its line of frozen foods. General Foods commissioned the manufacture of specialized freezer cases for the retail display and storage of their products. After years of small-scale market testing and local advertising campaigns, the drastically reduced preparation time and wide variety of frozen foods finally persuaded the American public.

In 1938, General Foods sold 150 million pounds of frozen Birds Eye products. National distribution began in 1940, but because the manufacture and purchase of refrigerators and freezers was halted during World War II, it was not until the consumer boom of the 1950s that the use of frozen foods became common. Since then, the frozen food sections of grocery stores have featured ever-increasing choices of delicious, nutritious food that can be enjoyed with a minimal amount of preparation time, allowing busy American families to eat well without spending hours in the kitchen.

Above, Clarence Birdseye experimenting with carrots; right, Clarence Birdseye inspects a retail display

The Klystron Saves Lives

Sometimes the invention of a single device can evolve into a wellspring of technology for other new and disparate industries. Such was the case with the klystron, a vacuum tube for generating and controlling ultra-high-frequency current. It originated as an electronics research project for solving an immediate problem — helping early pilots locate landing fields at night or through cloud cover. In this mode, it was the forerunner of modern radar, but it subsequently evolved into a medical technology that today is improving the quality of life for hundreds of thousands of cancer patients.

The klystron was invented by Russell and Sigurd Varian and their Stanford University associates during the summer of 1937 and was first known for its use in airborne radar during World War II. A launch pad for the founding of the company known as Varian Associates in 1948, this device also effectively launched the microwave industry, made possible worldwide communications via satellites and became the heart of high energy particle accelerators for both nuclear physics and medicine. Less than two decades after its invention and only a decade after the Silicon Valley company's founding, it became the heart of another breakthrough — Varian's linear accelerator, a 30,000-pound, 9-foot-tall machine designed to deliver therapeutic X-rays to cancer patients.

Today, Varian's modern klystron is still providing the pulse for the Clinac product line of medical accelerators. Around the globe, more than 3,000 such machines treat more than 80,000 cancer patients each day. Radiation therapy is a component of most hospital oncology departments and is considered the most cost-effective cancer treatment method available.

Clockwise from lower left: Sigurd and Russell Varian, Professor David Webster, William Hansen and John Woodyard with early klystron

From 50 to 60 percent of cancer patients in the United States receive radiotherapy at some point during their treatment. And today more people are surviving various types of cancer longer. In 1940 only one in four patients was alive five years after treatment. Today, with the many modalities available for treating cancer, including the medical accelerator, four out of ten patients can expect to live five years or longer. Because of the klystron, more of those who are diagnosed with cancer are not only surviving, but are leading fuller, more active lives.

THE SATURDAY EVENING

POST

MAY 29, 1943   10¢

BEGINNING—A NEW
KELLAND SERIAL
Heart on Her Sleeve

EDGAR SNOW
REPORTS ON GERMAN
ATROCITIES

Detail of *Rosie the Riveter*, by Norman Rockwell; opposite page, Consolidated Vultee workers applying an insignia to the wing of a PBY, San Diego, California, early 1940s

Manufacturing Helps Win the War

1 9 4 1 - 1 9 4 5

The nation was still waging war against the worst depression in its history when news flashed that Japan had attacked American forces at Pearl Harbor. Now a second, even fiercer war dawned. Ultimately, the United States would emerge victorious, but before it reached that point, it had to forge the weapons and wherewithal to become the "arsenal of democracy." As National Association of Manufacturers President William Witherow noted, "Victory on the battle front will be forged on the factory front."

The association itself worked indefatigably to help forge this victory. Even before the attack on Pearl Harbor, the organization inventoried nearly 200,000 factories, both large and small, as an early step in the mobilization of the nation's manufacturing sector. Once the United States entered the war, it continued to advise the government and began to counsel businesses with respect to meeting diverse wartime needs that ranged from the establishment of priorities and allocations, to the maintenance of worker morale.

Mobilization for the global conflict against the Axis powers required government and business leaders to put aside disagreements and to coordinate their efforts for the common cause. Businessmen flocked to Washington to serve as "dollar-a-year" men in war-related agencies; the government promised companies "cost plus" contracts that would cover production costs and yield a reasonable profit. Both government and business also agreed on certain fundamentals: civilian wants must give way to military needs; new facilities must arise and existing ones expand; vital raw materials or their synthetic replacements must be found.

Achievement followed agreement. Manufacturers changed their product lines faster than anyone could have imagined. By 1945 American industry had mass-produced 300,000 planes, 12,000 ships, 64,000 landing craft, 86,000 tanks and gargantuan amounts of munitions. The enlargement and conversion of factories and mills — their furnaces and assembly lines kept functioning by millions of workers, more than one-third of whom were women — had wrought this seeming miracle.

At the same time, industry had found ways to overcome shortages of critical raw materials, notably rubber, oil and various metals. Scrap drives and consumer rationing helped to make this possible, as did increased operating efficiencies and the discovery and subsequent mass production of remarkable synthetic products. Medical researchers were given a mandate to quicken their pace in the search for economical production processes for drugs such as penicillin. Interestingly, wartime production developed technological innovations that ultimately proved useful in peacetime, too.

Industry, in sum, had contributed immeasurably to the nation's victory in World War II, supporting the valiant efforts of America's armed forces. In turn, conflict and necessity had brought immense changes to industry. One thing was for certain: further extensive changes loomed in the conversion to a peacetime economy.

U.S. Factories Convert Product Lines and Help Win the War

The wartime partnership of government and industry resulted in the greatest production effort the world had ever seen — a decisive factor in the Allies' victory. Many of industry's leaders went to Washington to serve on boards that coordinated production of war matériel. From steel manufacturers to glass producers to paper products makers, firms converted their plants to wartime production. The massive economic mobilization finally accomplished the goal that had resisted even the most aggressive New Deal programs: ending the Depression.

During the conflict, American manufacturers produced more than $186 billion in airplanes, ships, guns and other equipment that made victory possible. Ford Motor Company, for example, built 8,600 bombers, 278,000 jeeps and 57,000 aircraft engines; Pfizer produced 50,000 billion units of penicillin in 1944 alone, half of the national total for that year; Boeing turned out more than 18,000 aircraft, including the B-17 Flying Fortresses and the B-29 Superfortresses. Not only did industry produce a great deal of wartime matériel, it produced that matériel rapidly, sometimes astonishingly so.

Parts and equipment came from every corner of the country. Some companies adapted their products for wartime use, while others moved into completely new lines of production. Automakers produced everything from airplanes to machine guns; General Motors alone produced 854,000 trucks for military use, the M-5 light tank, 2,507 Hellcat tank destroyers and 13,000 airplanes; Sherwin-Williams made paints for military use, produced a primary ingredient of an infection-fighting "sulfa" drug and also built an ordnance plant to manufacture shells;

a Firestone Tire & Rubber plant turned out anti-aircraft guns; a Maytag facility used its experience with washers to produce hydraulic units for the B-17 and B-26 landing gear and manufactured bomb bay doors and wing flaps, as well.

Along with conversion of manufacturing facilities and labor, the industrial leaders of the country converted their research efforts to solve the problems that had arisen out of the war effort. B. F. Goodrich worked to develop a simple solution to the wear and jostling of airplane

tires when they touch down. By creating a tire with wing-like vanes on the sidewalls, the wind passing the tires would, like a windmill, cause the tires to spin at 80 percent of the airspeed of the plane, thus assisting a smoother landing and reducing damage to the tires. Percy LeBaron Spencer, who never graduated from high school but patented more than 100 inventions while employed with Raytheon, invented the magnetron, a device that enabled radar unit production to soar from fewer than 20 per day to more than 2,600 per week.

The first nylon parachutes went into operation in 1942 — only four years after the discovery of the synthetic fiber.

It was this ability to drop everything to work for the common cause that assured the U.S. victory in the war, and the collaborative effort spawned many a future success in developing technologies.

Wartime production of Consolidated Vultee Catalinas, San Diego, California, circa 1942

Left, Sherwin-Williams paint applied to a 225-foot mine sweeper; above, grenades were painted inside and out

The NAM Contributes to the War Effort

The National Association of Manufacturers played a pivotal leadership role during World War II. Through special boards, conferences, committees and subcommittees, the NAM advised manufacturers, employees and politicians on how industry could help the U.S. win the war. Even before America became involved in the fighting, the NAM was on the leading edge of mobilization. In 1940, the organization established a National Defense and Mobilization Committee to envision strategies in the event of American wartime involvement. In early 1941, the NAM's "Preparedness Through Production" campaign assessed American mobilization potential. With help from its National Industrial Council, the NAM presented a report to the government on May 1, 1941, that inventoried the manufacturing sector's 185,000 large and small factories.

The NAM led the charge to mobilize the U.S. manufacturing base and also inspired the men and women in America's factories to produce the weapons that won the war, particularly through motivational efforts such as the "Soldiers of Production" campaign. Soldiers of Production rallies were held in communities nationwide, with NAM members delivering inspirational speeches on the paramount contributions American manufacturers were making.

The NAM used a variety of media to inspire wartime manufacturers. The "Defense for America" radio broadcasts were originally intended to be short-lived. Following the success of the first 13 broadcasts in selected radio markets, the NAM continued the shows and expanded the outreach to other radio regions. In a later series of radio broadcasts, NAM members discussed the foreseen challenges of reconversion. Members also spoke on short-wave radio to American soldiers in Europe and the Pacific. Throughout the war, the NAM conducted plant tours for journalists who had recently returned from the battlefront. The NAM also created posters, billboards and publications that informed and inspired workers.

The War Production Board sought the advice of the NAM on resource allocations and worker education. Throughout the 1940s, the NAM held joint conferences with the War Production Board and its predecessors. The government even asked the NAM for advice on how best to reorganize the War Production Board. NAM leaders and members testified before congressional committees on mobilization, productivity, price controls, reconversion and other issues. Countless NAM policy papers provided advice for legislators. With such a diverse membership, the NAM was in a unique position to maintain vital lines of communication between the manufacturers and the decision-makers.

Looking ahead to the inevitable complications of reconversion, the NAM realized that American manufacturers would need to be re-educated to produce in the postwar world. The NAM convened many postwar conferences to address manufacturers' needs and sponsored committees on postwar employment.

The NAM addressed the needs of America's rising stars on the factory floor: women. The organization had held "Women in Industry" meetings since 1926. To educate this vital part of the work force, the NAM held a "Women in War Jobs Conference" in Indianapolis in February 1943 and later held several conferences addressing the special postwar problems women were likely to face.

In the aftermath of the war, people worldwide recognized the significant contributions made by America's manufacturers. The NAM helped American manufacturers achieve their pledge that "Industry will build two battleships for every one that sinks. It will match every enemy bomb with a dozen. It will blacken the skies with planes to replace the ones shot down."

DEFENSE OF OUR LIBERTY BEGINS IN THE FACTORY

".. it all depends on you and me!"

© NATIONAL ASSOCIATION OF MANUFACTURERS

NAM Poster

Women Produce — And Women Change

Much of the necessary matériel could not have reached the war front in time had it not been for the efforts of an unprecedented 7 million women who joined the work force between 1941 and 1945. Performing all sorts of tasks that traditionally had been men's jobs, women drove buses and ambulances, worked in the fields and filled the factories that men entering the armed forces had vacated. At the height of the war effort, women comprised 37 percent of the work force in industries that were handling prime contracts.

Though women had enabled the tremendous output of military matériel during World War I, when the United States entered the war in 1941, only 80,000 of the women who applied for jobs were hired. Women proved vital to the war effort, however, and their ranks grew as industry recognized the valuable resource that had gone unnoticed for so long. The not-so-mythical "Rosie the Riveter" became a popular heroine, and women's presence in the factories enabled swift completion of military equipment: a bomber that had taken 200,000 "man" hours to finish now could be built in 13,000 hours.

Though many female employees were laid off or left their jobs after the war, the 1950 census revealed that more women were at work in that year than at any time before the war. Women had proven their productive capacity to themselves, their employers and society, and they had experienced the empowering effects of paid employment on a large scale. The incredible show of women in the work force during World War II began a trend that has accelerated with every decade.

Workers at Consolidated Vultee's plant putting the finishing touches on a USAAF Valiant

The U.S. Aircraft Industry Proves Anything is Possible

American industry, forging the sinews of war that made victory possible over the Axis powers, turned out vast quantities of war matériel, among them state-of-the-art fighters and bombers. U.S. production figures for aircraft astounded the world. Some industrialists were skeptical when President Roosevelt called for the production of 60,000 aircraft in 1942: not only was that goal met, but the number produced grew to 86,000 in 1943, and total wartime output was 300,000 planes.

North American's P-51 Mustang destroyed almost 5,000 enemy aircraft in the European theater of operations; Boeing's B-29 Superfortress, named for its massive firepower, was able to range more than 3,000 miles. It wreaked devastation on the Japanese homeland and ultimately carried the atomic bombs that ended the war. The B-29 was the world's heaviest production airplane, and it incorporated many innovations. In spite of its size, it set records for the distance it could travel nonstop, once traveling 8,198 miles in a flight from Guam to Washington, D.C., in 1945. Lockheed produced close to 10,000 P-38 Lightnings, whose twin-tailed design won the Army Air Corps competition for multi-engine fighters, but their greatest claim to fame was as the first American-built fighter to shoot down a Nazi plane. The B-24 Liberator, designed by Consolidated, was produced in greater numbers than any bomber in history — 19,256 were built by Consolidated, Ford, Douglas and North American.

These tens of thousands of planes were powered and equipped with parts from factories all over the country. For instance, immense numbers of badly needed, radio-operated "proximity fuzes" that aided bombardiers in hitting their targets were produced. Two General Electric turbojets powered the nation's first jet plane, the XP-59 Aircomet, on its maiden flight in 1942, though the XP-59 was immediately retired to be used only for pilot training.

Quantity was one part of the production success story, but flexibility was an important factor, too. As a result of combat experience, the U.S. Army Air Corps wanted constant changes and modifications in aircraft, and manufacturers delivered them. The B-29 Superfortress, for instance, had the ability to reduce its artillery from four gun turrets in front and one cannon in the tail, down to only the tail armament, enabling a top flight speed of 365 miles per hour. It was in this configuration that the B-29s carried the atomic bombs. This flexible design allowed the Super-fortress to change into a hit-and-run bomber in the later stages of the war, when U.S. planes faced less of a threat from enemy fighters.

Accommodating this unprecedented demand for airplanes and related equipment, the number of people employed in the aircraft industry increased from fewer than 50,000 in 1939 to more than 2 million in 1943 — almost one-eighth of the work force.

Perhaps the greatest achievement of the airplane industry during these years, however, was the way in which the various aircraft companies — competitors in peacetime — worked closely and cooperatively. They shared production processes, tools, materials, innovations, contracts and recognition — and even produced each other's aircraft — to achieve seemingly impossible production goals. The rapid advances in aeronautics during the war inevitably created a legacy for air transportation. Heavier planes flew faster and farther than ever before, leading to commercial airliners that would routinely carry passengers across the oceans and ultimately to commercial jet aircraft. Airplane manufacturers and their suppliers can be justifiably proud of their legacy.

Above, Boeing B-29 Superfortress; opposite, Lockheed's P-38 Lightnings under construction

Above, Case tractor unloading machinery after D-Day on the beaches of France; right, Case's D1 tractor modified with armor plating for military use; below, jeep assembly line

Industry Develops Vehicles for a Mechanized War

The Second World War was the world's first truly mechanized war, and industry's production of massive numbers of jeeps, tanks and tractors substantially aided the United States and its partners. Jeeps, the invention of American engineer Karl Pabst, were in high demand, as they were "GP," or general purpose, vehicles (hence the name "jeep"). More than 600,000 jeeps rolled off the assembly lines by war's end. Wartime industry also produced a huge quantity of tanks, most notably the M-4 model, commonly called the Sherman. The latter's velocity, maneuverability and sheer numbers — nearly 50,000 were manufactured — contributed mightily to the Allied triumph.

Tractors also played a role in the Allied victory. For example, of the approximately 75,000 tractors built by Case during the wartime years, more than 15,000 went to the military. Some of these tractors were equipped with special armor and shielding. Others were made for high-speed (40 mph) desert operations, and a low-slung design was used on aircraft carriers to maneuver airplanes into place.

Many manufacturers faced the wartime challenge of dividing their efforts between the tasks of maintaining a reasonable position in domestic markets and producing the necessary war matériel. Perhaps no industry faced a greater dilemma than the tractor industry. It was essential for manufacturers such as Case to continue a high output of farming equipment to help boost food production for the soldiers overseas and the folks at home.

Astoundingly, Case did keep this balance, managing to produce up to the government limit of farm-bound tractors, while contributing specialized tractors, ammunition and B-26 wings to the war effort. (Interestingly, manufacturing was not the extent of Case's contribution to the war effort. About 200 Case employees joined the war as the 518th Ordnance Company for Heavy Maintenance. The 518th, which did not remain exclusively "Casers" for long, repaired the specialized equipment the industry was producing for the war and served as proudly in Europe as their counterparts in the factories at home.) Jeeps, tanks and tractors were just another important part of industry's contribution to the war effort.

Wartime Shipbuilding Reaches Legendary Levels

During World War II, American industry more than fulfilled its pledge that it would "build two battleships for every one that sinks." Indeed, industry achieved prodigious results in all aspects of shipbuilding and maintenance. The legend of World War II shipbuilding was the Henry J. Kaiser Company, which built 2,770 "Liberty" ships to carry matériel across thousand-mile supply lines and to replace those ships lost in action. By introducing prefabrication and assembly line techniques, Kaiser set records for speed in shipbuilding, producing Liberty ships in just 41 days on average and accomplishing the incredible feat of building one in only 8 days.

Another company that pushed through extraordinary building feats was Newport News Shipbuilding & Dry Dock Company, where eight 33,000-pound aircraft carriers were constructed within less than 30 months — an average of one every 90 days. Among these were such famous carriers as the *Enterprise*, *Hornet*, *Essex*, *Intrepid* and *Yorktown*. Much of the manufacturing of these craft was done at North Carolina Shipbuilding Company, a subsidiary emergency shipyard created expressly to help Newport News meet the demands of U.S. naval contracts.

The most voluminous output of ships came from the efforts of Bethlehem Steel, whose 15 yards completed 1,127 ships during the war. The company, to meet its optimistic president's pledge to manufacture one ship every day of the year, completed 380 ships in 1943 — and still found the capacity to complete repairs on 7,000 more. This flexing of the shipbuilding industry's muscles was proper training for the decades to follow, as naval ships have played a prominent role in resolving conflicts and peacefully representing U.S. interests around the globe.

Above, ship construction in Shipway 3 at North Carolina Shipbuilding, September 26, 1941; left, launching hull No. 171 at Henry Kaiser's Portland, Oregon, shipyard, September 27, 1941

War Prompts Development of Synthetic Rubber

Crucial to the war effort was the alleviation of severe shortages of strategic materials. Japan's attack on Pearl Harbor effectively ended America's access to Southeast Asia, the source of 90 percent of total natural rubber imports. A drive for scrap rubber from tires and other manufactured goods provided a stopgap measure, as did the rationing of gasoline to limit wear on rubber tires, but experts deemed the nation's rubber reserves insufficient for the task ahead.

DuPont and B. F. Goodrich had begun developing synthetic rubber products during the 1930s, but the production cost was much higher than for natural rubber. To produce enough synthetic rubber to meet wartime needs, the government built production plants, and rubber and chemical manufacturers operated them, pooling their knowledge to develop the new industry almost overnight. By 1944, the partnership of industry and government had produced more than 800,000 tons of this vital synthetic product, which at the time accounted for nearly 90 percent of all rubber used in the nation.

In 1955, the U.S. government sold its synthetic rubber plants to private companies. Synthetic rubber has continued to play a vital role in supplying the many industries that use rubber — particularly the tire industry, which generally uses varying combinations of natural and synthetic rubber. As a result of the wartime breakthrough, synthetic rubber is now cheaper than the natural material and is used more frequently.

Rolls of DuPont's neoprene, nine feet wide and 1/100th of an inch thick, are prepared for shaping into a solid material, 1949

New Technologies for Living Come From a Deadly Weapon

An innocuous code name, the Manhattan Project, masked the huge effort by the United States to develop an atomic bomb during World War II. The effort was unprecedented and monumental, by far the largest technological engineering ever attempted. In many ways it has never been surpassed. The Manhattan Project cost over $2 billion (at a time when the entire gross domestic product of the United States was only $150 billion) and involved over 600,000 workers.

Private industry played a crucial role in the development of nuclear weapons, devoting research and manufacturing facilities, workers and an incredible sum of brainpower. Though design and assemblage of the atomic bomb took place in Los Alamos, New Mexico, its components were built in factories all across the United States. Research on the gas diffusion and electrical operations used to separate U-235 from U-238, which took place at Oak Ridge, Tennessee, and at Columbia University in New York, employed components manufactured by companies that included Allis Chalmers, General Electric, Westinghouse and Chrysler. The program to build a plutonium bomb took place in Hanford, Washington, in a plant largely built by DuPont.

New materials were necessary to complete this astounding scientific achievement, and some of them found their way into everyday American life. DuPont, for example, secretly produced a costly plastic for the Manhattan Project. Used to make gaskets for use in the manufacturing of U-235, this plastic, Teflon, is today a household fixture. Officially the lowest friction solid in existence, Teflon is ideal for use in such products as artificial bones (where the friction

of human motion would quickly wear down another material), electrical insulation and spacesuits. In fact, Teflon is so slick that the biggest challenge scientists faced upon its introduction into commercial products was finding a way to make it adhere to the surface of the product. Once that challenge was overcome, Teflon made its way into the home as well in

the form of non-stick cookware.

The atomic bomb was first tested at Alamogordo, New Mexico, on July 16, 1945. Three weeks later, on August 6, an atomic bomb was dropped on the Japanese city of Hiroshima. On August 9 a second atomic bomb was dropped on Nagasaki. The two bombs killed, respectively, about 140,000 and

75,000 persons and quite certainly hastened the end of the war. Some continue to debate the morality of dropping the bombs to induce the surrender of Japan. What is beyond question, however, is that the atomic bomb ushered in a new era in the history of warfare and the future of many technologies.

The invention of nuclear weapons

was one of the biggest technological achievements of all time, a union of scientific genius, the resources of a government and a nation at war, and the practical capacity of American industry. It also demonstrated, like no other invention of the century, the dark side of modern technology.

Atomic bomb scientists at testing site near Alamogordo, New Mexico, measuring radioactivity in seared sand particles, J. R. Oppenheimer, considered the father of the atomic bomb, third from left, 1945

Innovative Refining Processes Increase Gasoline Supplies

Until the popularization of the automobile, the most desirable product manufactured from crude petroleum was kerosene. But the internal combustion engine and the growing use of electricity for lighting reduced the demand for kerosene at the same time the need for gasoline was growing. As demand soared, improved methods of refining gasoline from oil were pursued. A thermal cracking process was developed in 1913, but catalytic cracking, originally developed in France in 1928, produced higher-octane gasoline with less pressure. Frederick Eugene Jules Houdry, the inventor of the catalytic cracking process, received important American financial support, first from the Vacuum Oil Company — which merged with Standard Oil of New York in 1931 and became Mobil Corporation in 1966 — and then the Sun Oil Company. After many months of fine tuning, in 1937 the Sun Oil Company announced the success of the first refinery built specifically for Houdry's refining process.

World War II brought a huge increase in demand for aviation fuel, which needed a higher octane rating than automobile fuel, and Sun's new refinery at Marcus Hook, Pennsylvania, shipped out more than 1.1 million barrels of 100-octane gas each month of 1945. The war also prompted the rapid development of a process that improved on Houdry's, fluid catalytic cracking. Due to the new refining processes, the United States was able to increase its output of high-octane aviation gasoline sufficiently to supply 80 percent of the Allies' need for the fuel during the war.

Pure Oil (since merged into Unocal) advertisement celebrating the oil industry's centennial, 1959

Pipelines Take Energy Where It's Needed

Early in World War II, construction began on a 24-inch oil pipeline to carry crude petroleum from Texas to Pennsylvania to assure adequate fuel supplies for factories and for military use. Completed in 1943, the remarkable "Big Inch" pipeline extended 1,341 miles and was America's first large-diameter, cross-country oil line. Pipe-laying on this scale had become possible because of advances in manufacturing steel pipes, as well as the introduction and refinement of electric arc welding.

Within a year, a second major pipeline, called the "Little Big Inch," carried refined petroleum products from Texas to New Jersey. Following its completion, the two lines together transported about 40 percent of the crude oil and petroleum by-products received in the East. After the war, the nation's pipeline system continued growing to meet the increasing demand for petroleum as fuel and as raw material for the production of plastics and other synthetics.

War-related industries needed natural gas as well as oil. As shortages loomed, the Roosevelt Administration asked Tennessee Gas and Transmission Company (later to become Tenneco) to build a natural

gas pipeline from Agua Dulce, Texas, to Charleston, West Virginia, to be "completed in time for operation during the winter of 1944...in order to prevent interruption of war production." In spite of the rugged terrain to be crossed and the worst flooding in years, the project was finished a month ahead of schedule. The company had crossed 67 rivers, sometimes laying as much as 7 miles of pipeline a day. The pipeline was a triumph for both Tennessee Gas and the war effort, and it was followed by many similar pipelines that would supply the plentiful natural resources of the West to the cities and industries of the East.

Above, a Tennessee Gas crew prepares a pipe for laying underwater, Clear Lake, Louisiana, 1944; upper right, *the Line* magazine, established in 1946 to chronicle the activities of Tennessee Gas & Transmission Company

New Drugs Save Allied Lives and Conquer Peacetime Disease

Discovered by Great Britain's Sir Alexander Fleming in 1928, penicillin would not be used to treat humans until 1941, when methods for mass-producing it made it a practical and highly effective treatment for such ailments as pneumonia, rheumatic fever and strep throat. Because England was under daily bombardment, Britain depended on the United States to produce large quantities of penicillin during the war.

Pfizer, along with other large pharmaceutical companies, took up the challenge with great determination. The company decided that its field of expertise, production by fermentation, had the most promising outlook for producing bulk quantities of penicillin (typically grown as a mold). Though the government — which did not have the same level of confidence that Pfizer did — refused to help fund research along this route, Pfizer invested $3.75 million between 1941 and 1945 in the construction of a fermentation plant and refinement of the process that finally did provide the first mass-produced penicillin to the Allies and eventually the world.

Though it was possible to produce penicillin in relatively larger quantities, it was so desperately needed on the war front that domestic prescription of penicillin was forbidden by the government. However, Pfizer, until it was forbidden to do so, gave over its monthly allotment for research and testing purposes (millions of dollars worth of the drug) to desperate patients. The production process itself was legitimized by the breakthrough and benefited subsequent discoveries greatly.

More effective and less dangerous to use than quinine, atabrine (also known as quinacine) came on the market during the war years and received widespread use among troops and civilians suffering from malaria in the Pacific and Southeast Asian theaters of operation. The American bacteriologist Selman Waksman in 1943 discovered streptomycin, a drug heralded in the treatment of tuberculosis. Streptomycin helped to practically eliminate a public health problem that was responsible for the deaths of almost 60,000 Americans a year. Both during and since the war, these "wonder" drugs have proved a boon to humanity, improving the quality of life.

Penicillium spore

Calculations from a Room Filled with Vacuum Tubes

Attempts to construct a mechanical calculating machine began centuries ago. Charles Babbage foresaw the possibility of a mechanical calculating machine in 1834, years before the advent of the adding machine. The idea of paper tape as a means of communicating instructions to and receiving information from a machine was put into practice with the telegraph in 1858. With the advent of electricity, such communication with an electronic calculating machine seemed a real possibility.

By the mid-1940s, several semi-electronic computers had been developed, including Vannevar Bush's Differential Analyzer and the Harvard Mark I, designed by Howard Aiken in 1944. The Electronic Numerical Integrator and Computer (ENIAC), designed during World War II at the Moore School of Electrical Engineering of the University of Pennsylvania and completed in 1946, was a significant improvement over its predecessors.

ENIAC was the first fully electronic digital computer and required about 1,000 square feet and some 18,000 vacuum tubes to operate. This giant could perform approximately 5,000 arithmetic operations a second — a revolutionary capability at the time. Though the computer required significant preparation and setting of switches before beginning a set of calculations, its speed of operation made it the ideal choice for complex mathematical problems with many tedious calculations and construction of mathematical tables. It was initially used by the army to calculate firing patterns, but was adaptable to many other uses as well.

Manufacturers could see the possibilities of using computers to

enhance the performance and utility of machine tools. This idea, a form of numerical control (NC), involved using a numerical code or language to communicate instructions to machines on the factory floor. Though ENIAC's speed has been far surpassed since then by much smaller machines — which can perform 2 million times faster than ENIAC — the principles this early computer demonstrated successfully have found their way into every office, factory and plant in the nation.

ENIAC computer, University of Pennsylvania, 1945

Detail of *Fluid Catalytic Crackers* by Thomas Hart Benton; opposite page, DuPont advertisement for cellophane

CHAPTER SIX

Peacetime Prosperity and New Conflicts

1 9 4 6 - 1 9 6 0

The end of World War II initiated major adjustments at home as millions of G.I.s returned to regather the threads of their domestic lives. Ultimately, these changes both visibly and invisibly altered the nation and its lifestyles, and helped countless numbers in their quest to live the American Dream.

With the war over, families could refocus on improving the quality of their lives. Manufacturers helped to make much of this improvement possible. First, of course, they furnished jobs for returning soldiers. In small towns, especially, smaller manufacturers — sometimes family-owned — were often the employer of choice. Workplaces of every kind became safer. Beyond this, manufacturers helped make possible the massive-scale construction of new suburban homes in which young couples raised families, ending two decades of doldrums in the housing industry. The Baby Boom had begun. Manufacturers also provided a rich variety of consumer goods to make life more gratifying and — especially for homemakers — easier.

Overall, gross national product in 1960 was five times the level in 1940, and this prosperity was reflected in the tastes of the time. With a booming economy and more time on their hands, Americans gave leisure and travel industries a larger market. Television sets became commonplace, multiplying tenfold between 1950 and 1955, bringing movies, news, sports and other programs into American homes. Television became the medium of popular culture, as families gathered in their living rooms to watch shows which in many cases mirrored their own lives. Automobile production — in limbo during the war years — accelerated, leisure travel increased and by the end of the 1950s, automakers had begun development of a revolutionary "compact" car. Air travel for business and pleasure, while expensive, became routine. The chemical industry launched a host of products, including synthetic fibers that transformed clothing styles and tastes.

As Americans found new ways to enjoy their free time, manufacturers were developing new products that would save time. Inventions like the transistor and new products like the photocopier would soon alter everyday life.

While enjoying widespread material comforts at home, Americans found themselves involved abroad in an intense ideological and strategic struggle with the Soviet Union. The cost of waging the Cold War, which became a "hot" war in Korea in 1950, was continued preparedness. The U.S. was now the leader of the free world. This vigilance, in turn, further stimulated the economy and technological developments in defense-related manufacturing facilities from coast to coast.

Television Brings the World into America's Living Rooms

The postwar years saw an infusion of innovative American-made consumer goods and appliances into the home. Television, in particular, has had a far greater impact than even its creators could have foreseen. Not only did "TV" put the world in a box and bring it into American living rooms, it generated a new popular culture, a new way of eating and a new way of entertaining. Families could watch it together in the evening, after a hard day of work or school. Home builders gradually started adding family rooms to homes, basing their design around the likely placement of the television.

Advertisers could now reach millions, and television ad revenue quickly surpassed that of radio. National leaders faced a new scrutiny from the American public, who now could look into the eyes of their president as he addressed the nation.

It was during the 1950s that television became America's common denominator. Televisions were sold by RCA as early as 1939, but the price tag of $625, the fact that RCA did not have a license to broadcast commercially and the onset of World War II (when television manufacturing was banned) caused a gap of nearly a decade before TV would reach a mass market. This delay could not have helped the television industry more if it had been a carefully planned marketing ploy; when television was introduced soon after the war, there were ready buyers waiting. In 1946, the price of a television had dropped to $375, and many wartime experts on radar, which employed similar technology to television, were out of work and ready to contribute to the development of TV technology.

By the early 1960s, roughly 90 percent of the nation's households possessed at least one television set. Most of them were still black and white. Color television, initially too expensive to manufacture at a reasonable price and not compatible with black and white transmission, was first broadcast in the U.S. in 1954. But color sets would not outnumber black and white ones in American households until 1972.

The programming during the 1950s both created and recorded the flavor of a decade. Comedies such as "I Love Lucy" and "The Honeymooners"

proved enormously popular, as did athletic events. Serious programming — the McCarthy hearings, the Kefauver Crime Commission hearings, "Playhouse 90" — also reached wide audiences. In fact, television was becoming the primary source of news for many Americans.

The driving force behind the rapid growth and variety of these programs was the sponsors, manufacturers who advertised their products throughout the programs. "Soap operas," for instance, grew out of short serials the soap manufacturers, such as Procter & Gamble, ran to create interest in their ads and their products. Today's soap opera sponsors are still primarily manufacturers of household cleaning products.

When the enormously popular "64 Thousand Dollar Question" proved to be rigged, some viewers became disillusioned. Realizing the theatrical power of persuasion that television had, even the chairman of the Federal Communications Commission from 1961 to 1963, Newton Minow, referred to the medium as "a vast wasteland." Or, the other hand, Marshall McLuhan, author of several influential books on mass communication, asserted that television was creating a new type of society — a global village populated by people with a new view of the world.

The debate over television's social effects continues today. All agree, however, it has given people all over the world unprecedented instant access to critical moments in history, from the glory of a moon landing to the tragedies of war and assassination.

Opposite, top, Vladimir Zworykin with a cathode ray tube which formed the receiver of his experimental television,1929; opposite bottom, television for bus passengers, San Francisco, California, 1950; above, family watching television, 1950s

Manufacturing Enriches Leisure Time

The dramatic growth of the U.S. economy in the Baby Boom years put discretionary income in the pockets of increasing numbers of Americans. By the end of the 1950s, more than half the country's households had income beyond what was needed for basic expenses.

The unprecedented level of affluence not only led to increased home ownership, but also resulted in higher levels of spending on recreation, as Americans eagerly took to golf, boating, bowling, photography, backyard barbecues and other leisure activities. Increased sales of movie cameras manufactured by Bell & Howell, Eastman Kodak and others, allowed families to relive family vacations and special memories through "home movies." Gas-powered lawn mowers made yard work more efficient, and demand for new types of sporting goods rose.

Bowling presents a classic example of an area in which increased demand led to improved products, which led to still greater demand — and the Brunswick Corporation is a case in point. As bowling gained popularity in the 1940s and 1950s, Brunswick nudged the craze along by introducing changes to make bowling

more attractive to families — such as adding colorful accents and comfortable chairs — and then marketing these improvements to bowling center proprietors. In the 1940s, Brunswick also introduced "customized" bowling balls with holes drilled to fit players' hands.

Then, in 1956, Brunswick installed its first Automatic Pinsetter — AMF actually produced one several years earlier — that sold so fast the company raced to keep up with the orders. Efficient, reliable pinsetting machines helped the sport grow even more, making it more enjoyable for bowlers and allowing bowling centers to operate dozens of lanes at all hours without hiring as many casual laborers.

The bowling craze settled down a bit eventually, but companies like Brunswick have continued to bring innovative products to the sports and games Americans love. Whether it's sails made of a tough fabric like Kevlar, skis constructed with high-performance plastics or skates with an in-line wheel arrangement for speed and maneuverability, new materials and designs have enriched and expanded Americans' leisure activities.

Brunswick Automatic Pinsetter

Land's Polaroid: a Darkroom in a Camera

By the 1940s, photography was more than a century old, and its technology was well developed. After inventing the Kodak box camera in 1888, George Eastman had gone on to add further innovations that made photography far more accessible to the amateur. In 1947, another manufacturer continued this trend by developing instant photography.

Dr. Edwin H. Land, the inventor of the first synthetic light polarizer, is perhaps better known for creating a remarkable process by which a photograph could be processed "instantly" — in a single minute. A relentless hunter of "magic" solutions, Land took up a challenge presented to him by his three-year-old daughter to find a way to make photographs ready to view "now."

Land's solution was not to change the principles of photography, but to include all of the components for development of a photograph inside the camera — essentially making it a miniature darkroom. The image was exposed on one roll of film, and the push of a button pressed the image to a separate piece of "positive" film; over this double layer of film was then rolled a chemical solution. After 60 seconds for the chemicals to develop the image, the process was done.

Though Land's process never replaced the professional photographer's darkroom or the infinitely adjustable 35-millimeter standard camera, he put an astounding new tool in the hands of the general public, whose need for the instant capturing of images was fulfilled by the Polaroid camera.

Dr. Edwin H. Land

Tremendous Strides in the Fight Against Disease

The postwar era ushered in a golden age in pharmacology made possible by the considerable investment in research and development by America's pharmaceutical manufacturers. New drugs were prolonging lives, preventing and eradicating fatal diseases and helping to improve the quality of life for those being born into the modern age.

Following in the path of penicillin, a host of so-called wonder drugs emerged to enhance the quality of life by diminishing suffering and effecting cures. This new generation of antibiotics, such as Terramycin (Pfizer), Aureomycin (Lederle) and Chloromycetin (Parke-Davis) were manufactured and widely dispensed, relieving many suffering patients. Various new tranquilizers and antidepressants were providing safer, non-addictive alternatives; Darvon (Eli Lilly), for instance, replaced codeine in hospitals around the world.

Research in the field of human hormones offered several new solutions. Steroids, notably synthetic cortisone, progressed rapidly. Though the many applications of hormone therapies were not apparent at the time, the ability of companies such as Syntex to mass-produce synthetic steroids would fuel research at institutes like Sloan-Kettering and would lead to new treatments for many conditions from arthritis to infertility. Another revolutionary breakthrough occurred in 1951 with Syntex's discovery of norethindrone, the first orally active contraceptive, which provided an easy and effective way to prevent pregnancy and plan a family. "The pill" is also credited with playing a role in the sexual revolution of the 1960s by reducing the threat of

Above, Jonas E. Salk checks samples of virus-laden fluid used in the production of his vaccine, Pittsburgh, Pennsylvania, 1955; opposite, Salk administering his vaccine

unwanted pregnancies. By 1990, the Guttmacher Institute recorded that 28.5 percent of women in their child-bearing years were taking the pill.

No medical development of the decade, however, received more fanfare than the Salk polio vaccine. Poliomyelitis afflicted 50,000 Americans in 1952 alone, and 3,300 of these cases were fatal. After years of research failed to discover a cure, Dr. Jonas E. Salk of the Pittsburgh University Medical School formulated an anti-polio vaccine derived from the killed virus itself that in 1955 was successfully tested on more than 1.8 million schoolchildren to evaluate its effectiveness.

In 1956 Salk's vaccine was surpassed when Dr. Albert Sabin perfected an oral anti-polio vaccine that utilized the live polio virus. Both men, along with the American pharmaceutical industry, had not only made it possible to eliminate one of humanity's most dreaded diseases, they had established new hope in virus-based vaccines that led to other successful discoveries in the future.

American Express card, 1958

Credit Cards Make a Country of Good Customers

When a small group of investors in New York in 1950 introduced Diners Club, the first credit card offered to the public, they offered a new variation on one of the oldest business practices, the extending of credit for good customers. The history of this plastic cash began in the late 1940s, when American oil companies gave their manufacturing customers plastic identity cards.

Following the manufacturers' lead, individual gas stations or department stores offered credit cards for their own goods and services; however, Diners Club was the first to offer a general credit card to the public. Though as the name indicates, it was first primarily used in restaurants, the idea of banks themselves extending credit to their customers eventually caught on.

In 1958 American Express offered its first credit card. The same year Bank of America entered the credit card business with the BankAmericard, the forerunner of the VisaCard. A rival group of banks introduced what later became MasterCard in 1969. By 1965 there were 5 million cards in use, and the trend only gained momentum in the decades that followed. By the early 1990s, the number of cards in use had increased to 1.3 billion, or almost five credit cards for every person in the United States.

Whether the credit card is good or bad for the economy has been much debated. Its detractors argue that the prevalence of easy credit has cut into the rate of savings and encourages overspending. Others have seen the credit card as democratizing access to capital and as a harbinger of a cashless economy to come. Whatever its consequences, the credit card has permanently altered how Americans spend their money.

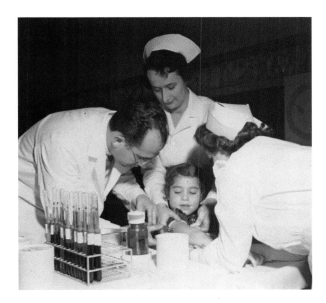

Office Efficiency Boosted by the Photocopier

A visitor to a nineteenth-century insurance company, law office or other business relying on written documents probably would have seen many people employed simply in copying records by hand. By the early twentieth century, somewhat fewer workers were required for duplication thanks to the typewriter and the use of carbon paper. But with all the progress of modern technology, most office workers in the 1940s were still copying documents two and three at a time. They were soon to be rescued from this tedious task.

In 1938, while working days and attending New York Law School in the evening, Chester F. Carlson invented an ingenious process for using electricity, rather than light, to produce a photographic image. This process was faster and less expensive than the contact photocopying processes then in use.

Carlson was able to transfer images by electrically charging a base plate to attract powdered ink (toner) to the outline of an image and then charging a blank piece of paper to attract the toner to it. The image was then fixed to the paper with heat. To distinguish it from photography, the process needed another name. Ultimately, "xerography" was accepted.

Amazingly, Carlson had difficulty finding a company interested in producing his invention. He was turned down by all the major companies he pursued, but the Haloid Company, in Rochester, New York, finally purchased his patents in 1947. The first xerography machines began to appear in a few offices in 1950. By 1962, the company, renamed the Xerox Corporation, saw its revenues reach $100 million. Carlson's brainchild brought revolutionary changes to office procedures and manpower needs and has become a standard fixture in offices.

Above, manufacturing copiers at the Xerox Corporation, Rochester, New York; top, the Xerox Copier, Model A, 1950s

The Transistor: A Tiny Foundation for a Technical Revolution

Jointly invented in 1947 by a Bell Labs team led by William Shockley, John Bardeen and Walter Brattain, the transistor heralded a revolution in electronics. Judging from a *Popular Mechanics* prediction in 1949 — "Where a calculator on the ENIAC is equipped with 18,000 vacuum tubes and weighs 30 tons, computers of the future may have only 1,000 vacuum tubes and perhaps weigh one and one-half tons" — the magnitude of the revolution could not be fathomed at the time.

The transistor was a sandwich of germanium or silicon which could amplify signals like a vacuum tube, but required less energy and less space. The foundation of nearly every electronics development that has followed, the transistor was first used by the military before it was produced commercially by Western Electric, a branch of AT&T, in 1951. During the following years, transistors replaced vacuum tubes in computers, and were built into televisions, radios, stereo systems, scientific instruments, aircraft systems and a host of other electronic devices. Eventually, transistors became building blocks for printed circuits, integrated circuits and computer chips, which have miniaturized electronics, enabling tiny computers to run everything from hearing aids to vacuum cleaners, and from electric guitars to automobile engines that can monitor and make maintenance adjustments for up to 100,000 miles.

The emergence of the transistor owes much to another pioneering phenomenon — the corporate research lab. Bell Labs, an autonomous group of scientists and staff jointly funded by AT&T and Western Electric, began unofficially in 1907 and incorporated officially in 1925. It was not the only such research organization: Thomas Edison, General Electric, DuPont, Kodak, General Motors and others had impressive labs by that time, as the number of private labs had risen from about 100 in 1915 to more than 1,000 in 1929. But Bell Labs has clearly been among the most productive. The secret of this productivity, crowned by the discovery of the transistor, was an innovative theory of management.

Bell Labs is one of the only commercial research ventures to be "unmanaged." Instead of the typical facility — in which business people determine research goals, quotas and funding — at Bell Labs, scientists are responsible for deciding what directions to pursue, and they pass this autonomy down to the individual researchers. Unlike research done at universities, the funding is an automatic investment, not dependent on research results.

The creative freedom this strategy accorded resulted in nearly 2,000 research contracts for the military and government during World War II. The research work done at Bell Labs has led to thousands of discoveries, including the facsimile machine, high frequency radar, the command guidance system used to guide unmanned space vehicles from earth, high vacuum tube amplifier and the solar cell. The list is astounding, and in the wake of Bell Labs' great success, thousands of Ph.D.s have congregated there.

Corporate labs continue to be a catalyst for new products and research developments, which promise even more astounding products in the future. For instance, the existence of superconductive magnets 78,000 times more powerful than the magnetic field of the Earth foreshadows the revolution that smaller, more powerful motors may soon bring from a research lab dedicated to making dreams of the future a reality.

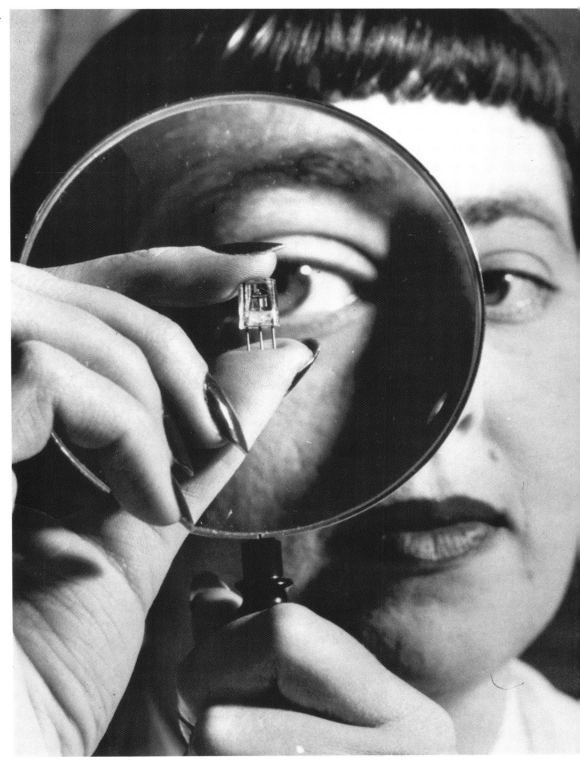

Research lab technician inspecting a new transistor, the revolutionary electronic amplifier

Computers Begin to Change the Workplace and the World

Foremost among the new technologies that helped to bring unparalleled economic prosperity and global leadership to the United States was the computer. Along with their revolutionary capabilities, early machines like ENIAC consumed gigantic amounts of electronic power, took up valuable storage space, were exceedingly difficult to program and frequently broke down. Occasionally a moth was drawn to one of thousands of vacuum tubes, causing a "bug" in the operation of the system.

Postwar technology engineered major improvements. The invention of the transistor led to smaller, more efficient, more sophisticated computers that could store millions of bits of data and perform thousands of diverse functions, but the larger mainframe computer was being increasingly adopted by business and government for larger number-crunching purposes.

The Remington-Rand Univac Division of Sperry Rand Corporation released the first commercially available stored-program electronic digital computer, UNIVAC (Universal Automatic Computer), in 1951. But IBM replaced Sperry Rand and its UNIVAC as industry leader when it launched its 701 and 152 computers in 1953 and 1955, respectively. Within a decade, "Big Blue" would command 70 percent of the world's computer market, although Sperry Rand and RCA, which in 1959 produced the first fully transistorized computer, were notable competitors.

The popularization of the computer depended less on proving its utility than on making its capabilities accessible to a wide range of users. The development of computer software and more

UNIVAC computer; Grace Hopper, creator of FLOW-MATIC, the first high-level programming language, second from right

advanced language programming, notably COBOL and FORTRAN (*formula translator*), helped people and computers communicate more clearly and led to better networking. As computers matured technically and became easier to operate, their

application spread universally, making unprecedented quantities of information accessible quickly and easily.

In almost all areas of human activity, people who had developed computer proficiency were discovering ways for the machines

to accomplish tasks and coordinate operations that had previously been impossibly complicated and time-consuming. In the 1950s, manufacturers were only beginning to explore the myriad uses of this highest species of the machine kingdom,

which has launched a revolution comparable to (or perhaps even greater than) the changes set in motion by moveable type and the printing press in the West.

Numerical Controls Redefine Factory Work

During the 1950s, American factories increasingly turned to automation to achieve increased production efficiencies. Numerical control, a term describing the automation of a machine tool by supplying it numerical "instructions," provided needed sophistication. Though many systems still used the punched paper tape principle established in the late nineteenth century, the increasing affordability and utility of computers had an impact in this field, as well.

Sometimes using tape, sometimes employing computers, numerical control made it possible to direct more than a hundred machine tasks simultaneously for lengthy periods of time and without the need for manual direction. The numerically controlled machine tool also had a more reliably accurate output than a manually operated machine, which depended upon the operator's skill and was therefore susceptible to human error.

Numerical control allowed manufacturers to relieve workers of the more tedious tasks, or those with particular safety concerns, and turn the machining work over to the machine with its set program of instructions. As a result, human workers could focus more on working out the problems of design, quality control and other evaluative decisions. Thus, increased automation brought not only greater manufacturing efficiency, but a drive for educational reform in order to develop the higher-order skills and technical proficiency modern workers need.

Giddings & Lewis' 54" Vertical Boring and Turning Mill, the world's first machine incorporating continuous path numerical controls for turning type operation; bottom, a paper tape reader.

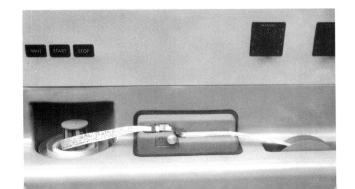

The Power of the Atom is Unlocked for Electric Power

The Manhattan Project unleashed the power of the atom as a weapon, but the "harnessing of the basic power of the universe," as President Harry Truman described it, had other uses. It went on to become a major source of electricity both in the United States and abroad. Beneficiaries of this clean, affordable energy included consumers and manufacturers, including the growing number of highly productive smaller manufacturing firms that were launched in the 1950s and 1960s.

The first experimental electric power derived from atomic energy was generated at Arco, Idaho, in 1951. Four years later, Niagara Mohawk Power first publicly offered this new source of energy, and in 1957 the nation's first large nuclear power station built for commercial use opened in Shippingport, Pennsylvania. In 1954, most commercial nuclear power development was placed in the hands of private industry, with the Atomic Energy Commission, established by Congress in 1946,

holding regulatory powers. (Today, those powers are held by the Nuclear Regulatory Commission).

The efficiency of nuclear power did not escape the military, either. In 1952 the United States tested its first hydrogen bomb and two years later launched General Dynamics' USS *Nautilus*, the world's first nuclear-powered submarine. The navy's first nuclear-powered aircraft carrier, the USS *Enterprise*, built at and launched from Newport News Shipbuilding in 1960, wasn't refueled until 1964. The

first nuclear-powered ship to enter combat, she is now a dignified old lady next to her modern counterparts in the *Nimitz* class, which can travel for a million miles (more than 15 years) before refueling their two reactors.

As new applications for nuclear power are being explored, research continues on ways to produce nuclear energy without depleting the world's supply of uranium-235 and to realize the atom's potential for producing cheap, safe, abundant energy.

USS *Enterprise*, the Navy's first nuclear-powered aircraft carrier

Roots of the Space Age

The Space Age is commonly viewed as having begun in the early 1960s. Yet it was manufacturers' achievements in the postwar years, coupled with the challenges posed by the Soviet Union's *Sputnik* launch in 1957, that made our nation's entry into the space race both possible and inevitable.

Following World War II, the United States, as the principal foe of communism and leader of the free world, embarked upon a program to maintain military superiority over the Soviet Union and its allies and thus protect U.S. security and vital self-interests.

The need for military superiority during the Cold War eventually led to some of the greatest developments in aerospace history. The initial steps towards manned space flights were taken in the late 1940s by pioneering test pilots who subjected themselves to incredible danger and discomfort to probe the limits of flight. Though jet planes in the mid-1940s were approaching the speed of sound, none had enough power to break through the sound barrier or enough strength to withstand the air pressure at that speed.

The first supersonic flight was piloted by one of aviation's greatest legends, U.S. Air Force Captain Charles E. "Chuck" Yeager. On October 14, 1947, he flew the X-1 rocket plane to a speed of 670 mph and an altitude of 70,140 feet. (At sea level, the speed of sound is about 740 mph, but sound travels more slowly at higher altitudes.) The plane, made by the Bell Aircraft Corporation, was rocket powered but was launched from a B-29 bomber so all its fuel could be used for flight.

Initially, aircraft designers built upon the success of the X-1 to produce military aircraft. Supersonic

Chuck Yeager and his X-1 rocket plane, the *Glamorous Glennis*, 1949

jets like North American's (now Rockwell International) F-100 Super Sabre and bombers like Convair's B-58 Hustler were manufactured in the fifties to meet the country's defense needs. This technology that the American military contractors pioneered paved the way for future development of civilian transports. In the late sixties, Russia's Tupolev Tu-144 and the British-French Concorde appeared. Although the use of commercial supersonic transports (SSTs) remains limited — military pilots are much more likely to exceed Mach 1 (the speed of sound) than their commercial counterparts — the scene has been set for supersonic

commercial service to become as common as subsonic travel is today.

Research and development also progressed on rockets and missiles, which quickly became an integral part of the nation's military arsenal. As early as 1949, the United States launched a guided missile 250 miles into space, the highest altitude yet reached.

Space-related research became a top priority of the U.S. government in 1957, when the Soviet Union launched into orbit around the earth the world's first satellite, *Sputnik* (meaning "travelling companion"). Fearful that its foe might subsequently be able to deploy long-range missiles armed with

nuclear warheads, the United States stepped up its own research and development programs. By the following year, the National Aeronautics and Space Administration (NASA) was created and *Explorer I*, the first American satellite, was placed in orbit. The Cold War had stimulated a space challenge that America's scientists and aerospace industry were determined to meet. Later in 1958, Convair's Atlas rocket proved its reliable strength as it powered an intercontinental ballistic missile more than 6,300 miles.

This show of technological strength revealed the possibility of sending into space larger, more

complicated satellites that could change what the average American saw, heard and knew about the world. Numerous satellites, including ones used to ascertain weather conditions, became operational before the fifties ended, and in 1960, AT&T applied for a permit to launch the initial commercial communications space satellite, the first in the network of satellites that has made possible the live broadcast of the Olympic games around the world and the view of Earth from the heavens on the evening news.

Detail of *Label Painting*, a collage of scanner bar-code labels by Tony Ligamani; opposite page, a footprint left behind as evidence of man's first walk on the moon during the Apollo 11 mission, 1969

CHAPTER SEVEN

Information Alters an Age

1 9 6 1 - 1 9 8 0

Enormous problems and challenges continued to face Americans as the second half of the twentieth century unfolded. Cold war tensions persisted, leading to a prolonged conflict in Vietnam, the most divisive war (the Civil War excepted) in America's history. Meanwhile, college campuses and urban ghettos erupted into protest and violence over war, civil rights and other concerns. Labor walkouts, by the late 1960s, were again on the rise. The turbulent sixties passed into history, but the concerns the decade had raised did not. Questions of poverty, drug abuse, crime, urban decay, uncontrolled inflation and empowerment of women and minorities, as well as government scandals, proved painful and perplexing. Americans also began asking government, industry and others to take a more active posture in protecting the environment.

Other profound changes affected the economy. An Arab-sponsored oil embargo following the Yom Kippur War of 1973 fueled tempers, prices and inflation. Long the industrial leader of the world, the United States saw its position gradually eroding. Alarmingly, it became a debtor nation, creating painful problems and portending more serious ones. Government regulation, for example in energy policy, often exacerbated existing problems. The period concluded with the lengthy Iran hostage crisis.

On the other hand, American industry also enjoyed astounding triumphs during these years. The space program, in particular, produced incredible feats, none more awesome than the Apollo 11 spacecraft that brought Neil Armstrong and Buzz Aldrin to the moon in July 1969, with six hundred million people — almost one-fifth of the world's population — watching live via television. Advances in telecommunications, from orbiting satellites to the laser, made earlier advances seem almost child's play in comparison, as did the breakthroughs in medicine, from CAT scans to new pharmaceuticals to artificial insemination.

Life expectancy, just 54 years in 1920, reached 70 years in 1965 and continued to rise. Science and technology also plunged oceanic searches to new depths. Concerns about energy efficiency prompted manufacturers to build more fuel-efficient vehicles. Manufacturers also continued and enhanced two of their most admired activities — corporate support of worthy charities and company research and development efforts that were the catalyst for many of the era's breakthroughs (though U.S. R&D growth trailed that of Japan and West Germany).

In all likelihood, however, the most extraordinary of all these technological advances, in terms of its immediate and widespread utility, was the computer, which was revolutionizing at dizzying speeds the ways people worked, played and even thought. Some viewed computerization as the most revolutionary advance since electricity. By the early 1970s, pocket calculators were bringing computing power into the home and classroom, making slide rules nearly obsolete. Change was becoming omnipresent, and one could only wonder what the world of tomorrow would bring.

Telstar Gives New Meaning to "Long-Distance" Communications

Satellite communications link the regions of the world today — and, as coverage of the first lunar landing showed, regions beyond this world.

The telecommunications industry was transformed in 1962 with the introduction of Telstar, a small satellite powered by solar cells, operated by computer and sent into orbit by AT&T. Linking the United States with Europe via television and radio waves, Telstar initially provided clear television pictures for as much as 20 consecutive minutes and simultaneously permitted the relay of as many as 20 transatlantic telephone calls. Later satellites could handle tens of thousands of calls at the same time.

The first satellite launched for commercial rather than government purposes, Telstar was followed by a host of communications satellites. In 1964, 12 countries, including the United States, established the International Telecommunications Satellite Organization (Intelsat) to develop a global commercial telecommunications satellite system.

Satellites do more than aid communications. From their orbits high above the earth, they also send back images that help to forecast weather, map remote regions and relay signals to ships and airplanes for navigation. Through these satellites, earthbound observers can monitor and contact all corners of the planet and gain knowledge about the globe that was inaccessible to earlier generations.

Telstar I, the first active communication satellite, an AT&T project

A Walk on the Moon Changes Earthbound Lives

Few if any events in history have stirred humanity as did Neil A. Armstrong's walk on the moon on July 20, 1969. The triumph followed dramatic acceleration of U.S. efforts to explore space that occurred during the 1960s. Various spacecraft, both with and without astronauts, defied the imagination as they probed far beyond earth.

Humans first ventured into the lowest fringes of space in 1959 in North American's X-15, a manned rocketplane that ultimately reached altitudes as high as 67 miles and speeds greater than 4,500 mph. The three X-15's that were built made nearly 200 flights between 1959 and 1968 under the control of military pilots who were considered the first astronauts.

The major thrust of the U.S. space program moved through three stages and was aimed at placing astronauts on the surface of the moon. The first stage, Project Mercury, beginning in April 1961 and ending in July 1963, took six astronauts on suborbital and orbital solo flights. The first American in space, Alan B. Shepard, Jr., journeyed on Mercury 3 (named *Freedom 7*).

The second stage, Project Gemini, encompassed 12 flights from March 1965 to November 1966 of two-man teams that could maneuver the vehicles for operations such as link-ups with other spacecraft (the Mercury flights had relied on automatic controls). Astronaut Edward H. White II became the first American to "walk" in space when he exited the Gemini 4 capsule on the end of a gold-coated cable and described to his partner in the spacecraft, James A. McDivitt, the view of the California coast far below.

Project Apollo was the final step in the reach for the moon. The program began tragically when a launching-pad fire on January 27, 1967, took the lives of the three astronauts on Apollo 1. The next manned Apollo mission was delayed until October 1968. It was the fifth manned Apollo flight, aboard Apollo 11 (called *Columbia*) that orbited the moon with astronaut Michael Collins aboard while a lunar module carried Neil A. Armstrong and Edwin E. "Buzz" Aldrin to a landing spot on the moon's Sea of Tranquility. Almost as amazing as the flight itself was the fact that millions of people all over the world watched Armstrong's first incredible steps on the moon via a live television broadcast, thanks to communications satellites.

None of these heroic deeds would have been possible, however, without the extraordinary technology designed and developed by industry. Every aspect of the space program — from the dehydration and special packaging of the astronauts' food, to the high-pressure gases piped in to flush the launch pad and the powerful Saturn C-5 booster that weighed as much as a light naval cruiser and that rocketed Apollo 11 into space — brought out the best in American industry.

The Apollo program culminated in Armstrong's feat, but further explorations took place during the 1970s. In 1976, the spacecraft *Viking I* landed on Mars and sent back photographs of the "red planet" to earth; three years later *Pioneer II* reached Saturn. Future developments, such as special ceramic tiles, would bring NASA closer to its new goal of designing a multi-flight craft that could return to earth intact, sustaining little damage from the blistering heat of reentry through the atmosphere.

As our exploration of space continues, one can only guess at its ultimate effect on human lives. President Richard M. Nixon indicated the magnitude of the space program's potential in his message to Armstrong and Aldrin on the moon when he said, "Because of what you have done, the heavens have become a part of man's world." The research associated with space flight has brought, or promises to bring, results ranging from the prosaic (new materials for everything from cookware to airplanes) to the fantastic (migration to other planets) to the awe-inspiring (learning the secrets of the universe — and whatever lies beyond).

Astronaut Buzz Aldrin posing for a photograph beside the deployed flag of the United States during the Apollo 11 flight of 1969

Jumbo Jets Make
Air Travel Commonplace

Family vacations once took people to another corner of their own state, or perhaps a neighboring state, with international travel a luxury that only the most affluent could enjoy. Today, it's not unusual for a family to venture to other countries for vacations, for students to expand their education by traveling or for businesspeople to meet with associates around the globe on a moment's notice. Such mobility was brought about by the development of jumbo jets.

Supersonic commercial aircraft debuted in 1969 with the test flight of the Concorde, the product of a joint Franco-British effort, followed by the first flight of paying passengers seven years later in 1976. After some initial interest in this exclusive new transport, the American aviation industry abandoned plans for its own supersonic carriers and concentrated on building quality jet planes that could service the public more economically. It was a wise choice: not many people in the world have had the means or the opportunity to break the sound barrier, but millions of Americans have flown in a jumbo jet.

Boeing introduced the first of its 747 models in 1970 — wide-bodied "jumbo" jets that could comfortably seat approximately 500 passengers. These leviathans are not only far larger than earlier commercial airliners, they're also more comfortable and less expensive to operate. The high-bypass engines — some of which are made by Pratt & Whitney, others by General Electric — deliver more thrust with less fuel than conventional turbojet engines, so that the planes fly farther without refueling. The jumbo jets were designed with multiple backup systems for greater safety, and despite their size

and power, there is very little noise inside the cabin.

The first jumbos, the 747, DC-10 and L-1011, were introduced at a time when air travel was growing in popularity at a rate that was outpacing airports' handling capabilities. Families wanted to see the world that came to them on TV, and U.S. businesses wanted to cultivate international partnerships and export markets. The carrying capacity of the jumbos accommodated the increased demand while reducing the need to expand or build new facilities and additional runways.

The United States airplane industry is also looking for new ways to make higher-speed travel a reality for commercial flights. With the use of supersonic planes limited because of the sonic boom they produce, visionaries in the industry look toward possible development of a hypersonic transport — traveling at six times the speed of sound. Should it ever become reality, the increase in human mobility that air travel promised when Lindbergh landed in Paris will reach incredible levels. Such planes would continue what the jumbo jets began: opening up every corner of the world to the average traveler.

Top, Boeing's 747-400 leading a Boeing 737; above, a 747 cockpit

The Interstate Highway System Spans the Continent

Many of the highways that cross this country offer a wonderful view — a precarious slope, a vista of rolling green hills. But the view as a highway twists between high cliffs that were once solid rock seems to feature not the rock, but the power of the highway itself. Many a child has marveled that the flat cross-section of a mountain was made by human efforts — and, of course, by powerful tools.

Impressed with the German autobahns during World War II, President Dwight D. Eisenhower urged Congress to appropriate funds to develop a similar system of four-lane, divided highways for the United States. Most American highways at that time were narrow roads that frequently took drivers through the most congested urban areas. Many existing roads

were large enough to handle heavier traffic but were difficult to navigate due to lack of adequate connections, signs and lighting. Improved roads and an easy-to-travel network were also essential for defense in case of war, the president further maintained. The passage of the Federal-Aid Highway Act, which secured funding for the National System of Interstate and Defense Highways via a gasoline tax, went virtually unnoticed by the public. In 1961, when the earth movers spread out across the countryside, however, the change began to look monumental.

As construction of new highways, repair of old ones, and design and construction of great numbers of interchanges began, great care was taken by the highway planners not to

disturb the natural beauty of the countryside and to select many scenic routes. Huge machinery, such as Ingersoll-Rand's Drillmaster blasthole drill, was necessary to cut winding passageways through the Rockies and the rolling hills of the Poconos. The Drillmaster, introduced in 1955, used a special "downhole" drill to dig close to the bottom of a blasthole, speeding excavation. The Crawlmaster, introduced in 1960, was just as powerful a drill, but it was lighter and smaller. This new design made the Crawlmaster a valuable tool during highway construction in the 1960s. By 1974, over 85 percent (or 36,000 miles) of the 42,000-mile system was accessible and in use. Along with machinery, other manufactured products such as

cement, steel and paint were essential.

The highway system provided the easy access and faster routes that made trucking, in many cases, the most efficient means of shipping manufactured goods across the country. The loops and spurs near metropolitan areas brought the suburbs closer to the cities. The highway has become a mythical place to Americans, symbolic of the vastness of the country and the freedom in open spaces. Songs have been sung about it, and highway jargon has entered the dictionary to describe its unique features. Whether for aesthetic or the most practical of reasons, the highway system has changed if not what we do in life, at least how we get there.

Workers laying burlap over a newly laid stretch of concrete, Kansas Turnpike, Topeka, Kansas

A spool of fiber optic "thread" used to transmit voice, data and video communications

Communications Travel a Highway of Glass and Light

Light, one of the most common and powerful of all tools in the universe, had, until the 1950s, a very concrete limit. It could be reflected, refracted, separated, directed, filtered and blocked; but it was not until the advent of the optical fiber that light could be carried along the curves of the ocean floor or the inside of the human body.

The optical fiber and its properties were discovered in the 1950s in England and subsequently developed for practical use in the United States. In 1974, Bell Labs invented a process for greatly reducing impurities in glass fibers, and three years later, AT&T transmitted the first television signals via optical fibers. Their development paralleled the advance of lasers, which are frequently used to create the light pulses that transmit information through optical fibers.

The optical fibers used today are thinner than a strand of human hair, yet capable of carrying immense quantities of information. For instance, four fibers in a transatlantic phone cable can handle 40,000 calls at once, compared with a single copper cable laid in 1983, which can carry fewer than 10,000 calls and is twice as thick. Optical fibers offer advantages beyond larger capacity. They are also subject to less electrical interference and need less amplification.

Fiber optics was developed just as the volume of information carried over wires was ballooning. This new technology has made it possible to utilize the tremendous potential of light for carrying information and has supported the rapid development of facsimile machines, computer links and various new media. Optical fibers have also been adapted for a number of industrial and medical uses. Medical instruments using these fibers enable physicians to observe internal parts of the body without surgery for both diagnostic and treatment purposes. In the future, they may provide a means to power computers by light rather than electricity, and they already have become vital supports for the Information Age.

The Power of Light Goes to Work

Some inventions revolutionize a specific area or industry; lasers have had profound effects ranging across many fields. They're used for precision cutting in industry and in surgery; they create holograms and read bar codes at checkout counters; they measure fault shifts in earthquake zones and propel light through fiber optic cable; they read compact discs and measure the distance to the moon.

The discovery of microwave amplification by stimulated emission of radiation (masers) in 1953 by Columbia University Professor Charles H. Townes made it possible, among other things, to increase extremely low sounds in radio communication. It also propelled the quest for a similar breakthrough in optics: a single-frequency, coherent beam of light that could deliver enormous energy to a small area. Albert Einstein had correctly explained the principle of the laser in 1917, and Arthur Schawlow had proposed, in 1958, amplifying light through the same methods used to amplify microwaves. It was Theodore Maimann, however, at Hughes Research Laboratories in Malibu, California, who built the first practical laser (light amplification by stimulated emission of radiation) in 1960.

In the years that followed, lasers both enhanced existing technologies and enabled the development of new ones. Compact disks (CDs) and, to a lesser extent, videodisks surged in popularity — the former outselling cassettes by 1991 — and improved the sound quality of music in Americans' homes. CDs are now the heart of CD-ROM multimedia computer applications.

Holography, the storing and displaying of three-dimensional images, represented another new application of the laser, finding use in the fields of art and jewelry, counterfeit prevention, and assorted scanning and range-finding devices. Laser printing of extraordinarily fine quality was offered by firms such as Hewlett-Packard. In medicine, the laser has proven of inestimable value in eye surgery and in the removal of both benign and malignant tumors. The laser has opened new doors in many manufacturing fields, and industry will continue to find exciting new applications for this invisible workhorse of modern technology.

Above, modern laser cutting, Alabama Laser Technologies; right, RCA scientists testing 10-watt argon gas for NASA's earth-to-space communications experiments, 1967

The Microprocessor Combines Computing Power and Affordability

While computers had benefited greatly from the transistor, the miniaturization of electronic components had just begun.

Integrated circuits with thousands of individual transistors made possible vastly more sophisticated computing operations. Further, these integrated circuits increasingly consisted of silicon chips, which were able to withstand far higher temperatures than their germanium chip predecessors. In 1971 Intel marketed the microprocessor, a miniature integrated circuit contained on a single silicon chip, which could perform several functions as efficiently as — and more cheaply than — much larger computers.

These developments marked a new phase in society's relationship with computer technology. As computers got smaller and less costly, they became more accessible. The largest computers, notably the Cray-1 supercomputer, which was designed for

Control Data in 1958 and was the first totally transistorized computer, were of vital importance for the military and for such operations as continuous-process manufacturing and aircraft design, but their prohibitive costs limited their accessibility.

A challenge to these large mainframe computers was foreshadowed in 1977 when two college students, Steven P. Jobs and Stephen G. Wozniak, founded Apple Computer and soon introduced Apple II, a much less costly computer designed as much for personal as for institutional use. It became evident that the PC was no mere passing fad. IBM introduced its own personal computer in 1981 and others followed. Since then, nearly every segment of the population has benefited from the ability of computers to increase productivity in tasks as diverse as balancing a checkbook or designing metalworking patterns.

Intel's 8008 processor

Manufacturers Adopt Old and New Production Strategies

In the 1970s and 1980s, as American industrial hegemony was challenged by inroads of foreign competition, many industrialists turned to Japanese production methods to study the "secret" of Japanese success.

Two of the techniques that were most avidly implemented were "just-in-time" manufacturing and "total quality control." Ironically, both of these methods had been touted to postwar Japanese industry by American management experts, who had to some extent remained prophets without an audience in their home country until the 1980s.

"Just-in-time" production involves minimizing excess inventory costs by tailoring the manufacture and procurement of components that are needed in small lots and short lead-time, while eliminating superfluous aspects of the work process. This complemented the notion of "total quality control," introduced by W. Edwards Deming, of raising the level of the quality of manufactured components to the highest possible standards by promoting a sense of cooperation among work teams. Both ideas were adopted with much fanfare by American manufacturers in the 1980s. While neither is a panacea, they are both examples of the creative adaptations that many American manufacturers are adopting to prosper in a world of global competition.

Just-in-time deliveries keep OshKosh B'Gosh cutting tables supplied with the right fabrics at the right time

Microwave Ovens
Change Meal Preparation

The microwave oven, patented in 1946, evolved from World War II military experiments involving radar, but it took a melted chocolate bar to propel the invention into everyday use. The microwaves emitted from a magnetron (the main component of radar) excited the water molecules in the chocolate bar in Percy LeBaron Spencer's pocket. Looking at his melted chocolate bar, he realized that the heat given off by these water molecules could be used to heat all kinds of food.

Originally called the Radarange, the first available model, introduced by Raytheon in 1953, weighed 750 pounds, stood 5 1/2 feet high and cost $3,000. Designed for larger users such as restaurants, railroads and ships, the Radarange gradually was modified into the microwave oven — cheaper, more compact and a fixture in numerous American kitchens. Amana Refrigeration, Inc., introduced the countertop microwave oven in 1967. As new food processing and packaging methods evolved to take advantage of the microwave's capabilities, it became possible to prepare many foods in a fraction of the time required by traditional cooking methods. With increasing numbers of dual-income households, the microwave was a welcome addition in American homes (even more popular than the dishwasher), where the convenience of cooking a meal in minutes provided new flexibility.

Raytheon's Radarange demonstration, Waldorf-Astoria Hotel

Food for a Faster Generation

The creation of the hamburger, like many of the great inventions of twentieth-century America, is the source of dispute. One likely claimant, Walter Anderson, assembled his first hamburger sandwich in a Wichita, Kansas, cafeteria in 1916. Five years later, Anderson and E. W. "Billy" Ingram opened the initial White Castle restaurant in Wichita, ushering in the era of the fast food chain restaurant. But it was only after World War II that the fast food restaurant came into its own.

A new American tradition began in 1955 when a visionary named Ray Kroc opened his first franchise and in 1961 bought the McDonald brothers' burger business. McDonald's would soon emerge as the largest of all fast food chains, with over 15,000 restaurants in more than 80 countries by 1995. With a hot Egg McMuffin waiting, commuters had access to a morning meal on the run, and a family could enjoy a hot, tasty meal for a reasonable price.

In an era when the Big Mac is used as an index for inflation, the fast food restaurant is clearly one of the most distinctive creations of postwar American capitalism and the food manufacturing industry. Fast food is the product of an era when developing convenient products and services that simplify people's lives has been an important aspect of technological innovation.

McDonald's first restaurant, 1950s

Detail of *Made in America by* Peter Max, part of a series for The National Association of Manufacturers' centennial; opposite page, racks of bottles containing genetically engineered cells at Amgen, Inc.'s mammalian cell culture facility

Modern Challenges and Opportunities

1981 - PRESENT

In spite of technological progress, by the early 1980s, dark clouds seemed to be gathering on the industrial horizon. New competitors in Europe and Asia were threatening American manufacturers — even in some of the industries that traditionally provided America's backbone. Detroit was looking anxiously over its shoulder, as were big steel and many electronic firms. The foreign trade deficit rose dramatically. In addition, the domestic market was changing, and the increasingly diverse nation seemed to be splitting into small niches of consumer interest. Further, manufacturers increasingly were plagued by unnecessarily stringent labor and environmental regulations. For example, Congress had adopted 59 key labor laws since 1900, and enacted 21 more in the 1960s — and others still in the years that followed. As global competition rose, manufacturers became less able to pass on the high costs of regulation through higher prices.

In the mid-eighties, however, a turnaround began that gained momentum in the 1990s and restored industry's luster. Recognizing that change was here to stay, American manufacturers responded to the challenges with the innovative spirit that has been its hallmark, creating new kinds of organizations and processes. The employees of American industry proved their worth as a more efficient and quality-conscious work force than foreign competitors. As a result, American industry emerged as the most productive in the world, at the cutting edge of technology.

The electronic revolution reached into virtually every household during the period, though consumers might not have fully realized how computers were affecting their everyday life. The personal computer and increasingly "user-friendly" software facilitated the spread of computer literacy. Millions of Americans used personal computers at work, at home and in the classroom — providing vital, early computer exposure for the leaders of tomorrow. Microprocessors were placed in a myriad of machines. Most people were at least vaguely aware of the role these tiny computers played in their new cars, but how many realized that many of their appliances, like vacuum cleaners and washing machines, depended on microprocessors as well?

The eighties and nineties also saw the continued technological transformation of the factory floor, with increasing application of automation systems like computer-aided design (CAD), computer-aided manufacturing (CAM), just-in-time inventories and — at the most advanced reaches of automation — computer-integrated manufacturing, which extends computer control over the entire flow of work in a plant.

Communications innovations likewise swept through homes and workplaces. Facsimile machines, modems, electronic mail, cellular phones and the development of electronic networks and media — the "Information Superhighway" — offered virtually instant access to people and information, with manufacturers responding quickly to new opportunities. (For example, four optical fibers, each thinner than a human hair, placed within a cable can handle 40,000 transatlantic phone calls simultaneously.)

Perhaps the biggest victory of the era was the end of the Cold War and the collapse of many of the world's communist dictatorships. Many factors played a role, but America's commitment to being the world's premier economic and military power, and the contributions of the nation's defense products manufacturers cannot be underestimated.

News stories about technology began to sound more and more like science fiction — but they were real. In medicine, bioengineers built machines that provided the first look inside the human body and that replaced defective organs with artificial ones. Genetic engineers learned to manipulate the building blocks of life itself. New medical instruments and drugs revolutionized the treatment of arteriosclerosis, heart disease, cancer, hypertension, ulcers, cataracts and more. The expected length and quality of life continued to rise.

Manufacturers' success extended to labor and environmental issues as well. Due to employers' consultative efforts to increase workplace safety and overall employee satisfaction, union membership dropped to only 11 percent of private sector workers. Manufacturers have also improved environmental quality and adopted pollution-prevention programs. Since 1970, airborne levels of lead are down 98 percent; carbon monoxide emissions have been reduced by 50 percent; sulfur dioxide emissions are down 30 percent — even as coal use has nearly doubled; and current model cars emit an average of 80 percent less pollution than 1970 models. With a great concern for human and natural resources, American industry — through its innovation and productivity — reestablished its position at the forward edge of global competition.

Artificial Intelligence: Research Aims to Create a New Kind of Machine

Scientists are continually pushing the limits of computer capabilities. On the frontier of computer technology is artificial intelligence, or AI, which enables computers to think for themselves and communicate with the world directly, without the help of programmers.

Researchers in artificial intelligence are attempting to develop computer systems and programs that can duplicate various aspects of human intelligence, such as diagnosis and decision-making, pattern and speech recognition, computer vision and other processes of thinking and learning.

On the theoretical level, some visionaries suggest that as AI research seeks to imitate the human thinking process, it will lead to a fuller understanding of the human mind itself. On the practical level, AI has already been put to work in ways that deliver knowledge quickly and easily. One of the first practical applications of AI research has been the development of expert systems: computer programs that replicate human expertise and decision-making in a specific area. Expert systems are already at work in fields such as medical diagnosis, financial decision-making and geological prospecting.

Artificial intelligence also holds promise for the future of robotics. Robots, once featured only in science fiction, play a major role in many industrial operations today. The first practical robot worked in a General Motors plant in 1962. By 1992, roughly 400,000 were at work worldwide, and robotics was a $6 billion industry.

Though not the "mechanical humanoids" envisioned by Karel Capek, the Czech playwright who in 1911 first used the term "robot" (from the Czech word for "drudgery"), robots are capable of replacing human workers for certain tasks. They are particularly suited for jobs that are too monotonous, difficult or dangerous for people to perform. Robots, for instance, are used to repair defects inside nuclear reactors.

Robots have grown in sophistication as they have incorporated advances in computer technology. Cincinnati Milacron Corporation produced the nation's first totally programmable robot in 1973. Research in artificial intelligence promises to increase their capabilities dramatically by producing robots that can sense and operate intelligently in their environment.

"Thinking" robots and computers will surely have a multitude of applications. Most likely, they'll bring philosophical challenges as well, as humans work out new relationships with new kinds of machines.

Chrysler's Sterling Heights assembly plant, where cars are put together almost entirely by robot

CAD/CAM Marks a Turning Point in Production

Below, Carton Service, Incorporated's carton design process aided by CAD/CAM technology, Shelby, Ohio; bottom, a recording studio outfitted with Peavey Electronics Corporation's products, manufactured entirely by CIM processes

Near the beginning of the twentieth century, improvements in mechanization revolutionized manufacturing by making it possible to make products in immense quantities instead of one at a time. Computer-aided design (CAD) and computer-aided manufacturing (CAM) systems, which began to appear in the 1970s, have put the power of the computer to work on the factory floor. With CAD/CAM, manufacturers can respond to market changes and have all the flexibility of a craft-based business while benefiting from the efficiencies of mass production.

CAD allows both creation and testing of designs on a computer screen, with programs that are now sophisticated enough to check for accuracy and workability. CAD systems are used for almost all large or complex projects, as well as for intricate tasks that would be impossible for a person to complete, such as designing the tiny circuits in microprocessors and other integrated-circuit chips. Computer-aided manufacturing systems prepare instructions for automatic tools and control manufacturing processes, including the operation of robots. The most modern role of computers in manufacturing is evidenced in computer-integrated manufacturing (CIM) — the use of computers in every step of the design and manufacturing process. The sound equipment produced at Peavey Electronics Corporation is the result of Peavey's move to CIM technology. These systems have brought increased quality, speed, efficiency and flexibility to manufacturing.

Computers have profoundly affected industry's labor needs, leading to a decreased demand for unskilled workers and a heightened need for

technically sophisticated employees. By increasing the pressure to attain higher education levels and blurring the distinctions between "blue-collar" and "white-collar" work, new technologies such as CAD/CAM and CIM are altering the social fabric, as well as the factory floor, and helping U.S. manufacturers prevail in the global marketplace.

Personal Computers Transform the Workplace

"Less is more" could be the motto for much of the computer industry. Just as the electrification of household appliances brought a new standard of convenience, the miniaturization of electronics, particularly computers, has presented Americans with a new standard of convenience, efficiency and productivity in the workplace.

Growth of the personal computer market was spurred by technology: between 1981 and 1995, the computing power of PCs doubled almost every two years. These smaller, cheaper computers were snatched up by businesses of all sizes, schools, libraries and families. During the 1980s and 1990s, as microprocessors made computers smaller and more convenient, many companies began to equip employees' desks with personal computers and train people in their use. Saving countless hours of labor, freeing employees from tedious tasks and dramatically increasing the efficiency of storage and retrieval methods, the PC has transformed the workplace, changing both the structure and culture of many corporations.

The vast amount of data and sophisticated operations the PC makes accessible have allowed many companies to give individual employees greater control and overall responsibility for tasks that used to be divided into numerous pieces and handled by several layers of employees. As a result, these companies have created more flexible, innovative and rewarding work environments, while cutting production costs at the same time. Microsoft and others have helped make the PC easier to use.

One of the greatest changes this new standard of convenience has effected is the location of the workplace itself. The commute to the office, for some, may eventually be a thing of the past, as the mobile office becomes a more widely adopted reality. Utilizing such technological marvels as the fax machine, cellular and portable telephones, electronic mail and the computer modem (as well as overnight delivery), some individuals can work as efficiently and effectively at home or on the road as they can at the office, and a business in the middle of Manhattan has fewer advantages over a business in the middle of the Wisconsin countryside. Already, the increasing opportunity to work independently is creating a highly flexible and entrepreneurial work force and, for many workers, both men and women, helping to reconcile the needs of work and family.

IBM's first personal computer

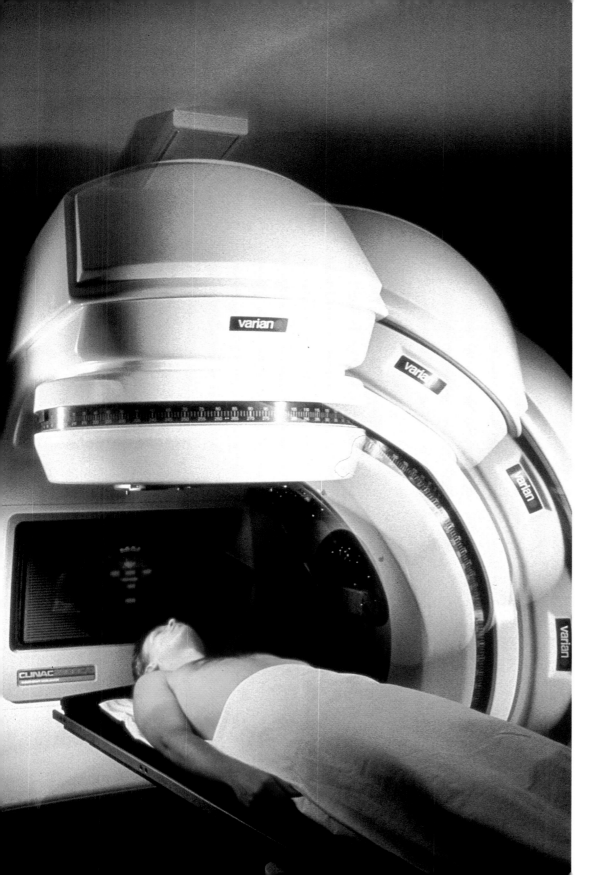

Medical Advances Lengthen and Enhance Lives

Medicine increasingly has used extraordinary imaging techniques to improve diagnostic methods. Meanwhile, the pharmaceutical industry has also continued to introduce vital new products to enhance the quality of life.

Since the advent of the CAT scan (computerized axial tomography; now known usually as computed tomography, or CT) in the 1950s, a host of more sophisticated devices has revolutionized diagnostic imaging, which can now see organs functioning, blood flowing and metabolic cellular changes. These include various types of scanners, radioactive tracers, thermographs and MRI. MRI (magnetic resonance imaging) uses magnetic forces that cause atoms to transmit radio waves that are then detected and recorded. CT and MRI scans have become fairly routine and highly useful imaging procedures, with CT the preferred method for looking at bones, while MRIs are superior at imaging soft tissues. Since it uses no nuclear materials, MRI is considered a safer technology.

If diagnosis is half the battle, the other half — treatment — is fought by new medical products developed from modern materials and the latest drugs from the pipelines of the American pharmaceutical industry.

Though bionics sounds like an exotic specialty, several million Americans each year benefit from advances in bionic science, which creates devices that perform human body functions. Researchers have made notable advances in finding metal, ceramic and polymer materials that are biocompatible with the human body. Cardiac pacemakers, artificial hips, synthetic skin, joint replace-

ments, advanced myoelectric prosthetic devices, Dacron blood vessels and other bionic parts are implanted in recipients, while devices such as the kidney dialysis machine and the heart-lung machine are used by patients on a periodic basis. The use of bionic parts adds another weapon to medicine's arsenal — one that can perform what once would have been considered miracles.

The costly and involved research and development processes that pharmaceutical companies maintain to keep their product pipelines full have been complemented by computers, as well. Advanced technical systems, including Cray supercomputers, now allow pharmaceutical companies to test new compounds more rapidly, thus reducing the time-consuming screening process and opening the door to potential new discoveries to fight pain, discomfort and disease.

Research efforts are investigating natural materials from around the world, as well as designing synthetic drugs. From the pipeline of Merck in 1987 came Mevacor, a highly effective drug to combat dangerously high levels of cholesterol. Shortly thereafter Eli Lilly brought out Prozac, a drug initially designed to combat compulsive behavior, but which subsequently has enjoyed enormous popularity as an antidepressant. In 1992, Procardia XL was marketed by Pfizer to relieve hypertension and angina and became the most successful cardiovascular drug ever launched. Thanks to modern imaging techniques, new medical products and instruments, and breakthrough pharmaceuticals, more Americans are able to enjoy better-quality health than previous generations could have imagined.

CAT scan in use, 1993

Genetic Engineering Creates Living Products

Since the discovery of the structure of DNA in 1953, the field of biotechnology has exploded, and research has already paid dividends for human health as well as agricultural productivity.

The human genome mapping project, searching for the location and identification of all 100,000 or so genes, has consumed an extraordinary amount of time and expense, but holds out the promise of immense rewards. Genetic engineering in humans has already improved lives and in some cases preserved them. Genentech cloned the first recombinant DNA product, human insulin, in 1978; the cloning of an ADA enzyme to save the life of a young girl with an ill-functioning immune system in 1990 represented the first successful human gene therapy.

Bioengineers are working on organ replication, including even the heart itself, to increase the available organs for transplants. Despite the staggering costs of research and development, the biotechnology industry continues to pioneer in the quest for new products to improve and to preserve human life.

Applied to agriculture, genetic engineering has produced such other seeming miracles as a frost-resistant tomato. Genetic engineering of plants has had far-reaching consequences for the farming industry and for the hungry mouths of the world. New varieties of wheat, corn and rice were developed during the 1960s to help poorer, overpopulated nations feed their people. This approach saved and improved countless lives throughout the world.

More recently, genetic engineers have changed the properties of some plants by inserting genes with desired properties, such as resistance to various pests. While insects can make rapid evolutionary changes, like developing a resistance to pesticides, the plants they feed on can be provided a more permanent type of protection through the assistance of genetic engineers. Monsanto's NewLeaf potato plant is protected by the presence of a particular protein in its leaves. Though this protein is harmless to humans, birds and even other insects, it is dangerous to the Colorado Potato Beetle, the largest threat to American potato crops. It is the first plant genetically engineered to resist a particular pest to be approved for commercial use, and with the EPA's approval in May 1995, this new potato has the same taste, look and nutritional value as the Russet Burbank potato from which it was developed.

Monsanto has also developed soybeans resistant to the most popular herbicide in the world, Roundup. The company is exploring corn and cotton resistant to insects, delayed-ripening tomatoes and produce protected against disease.

Though mass starvation was predicted a few decades ago, such advances have helped increase the earth's ability to feed its people safely and efficiently.

Above, genetically engineered cotton; right, a Colorado Potato Beetle

Small Manufacturers Help the Country Thrive

Small businesses have provided much of the dynamic thrust behind America's economy since the country's founding. In the early years, virtually all businesses were small in size. Manufacturing enterprises expanded with the increasing use of machines, which required considerable capital to acquire and produced more than manpower alone. In the late nineteenth century, with a more efficient transportation system linking the nation, readily available electric power and new management strategies, businesses grew still larger. The process has continued in the twentieth century

with a global business environment of mergers and international investment that is conducive to the development of multinational corporations.

However, small business remains the epitome of the American entrepreneurial spirit, and continues to play an integral role in economic growth. In fact, of the 19 million new jobs created during the economic expansion that lasted from 1983 until 1990, small businesses accounted for a healthy share.

Small and mid-size manufacturers play a very special role. Located throughout the country, they are often

world-class producers — among the best in their specialty. Their customers are sometimes the final consumer, occasionally the government and often other manufacturers who integrate their components into final products.

Smaller manufacturers must overcome a multitude of challenges, ranging from the disproportionate impact of unnecessarily burdensome government regulations to the simple diseconomies of scale that sometimes accompany being a smaller firm. But these same small and mid-sized manufacturers compensate with ingenuity

and the dedication of both their ownership and work force. Many have legacies dating back decades, and they are often viewed as among the best places to work in their local communities, where they also tend to be very active in civic and charitable causes. Today, thousands of small manufacturers with foresight are exporting their products abroad, truly competing in global markets.

In the intensely competitive markets small manufacturers are now facing, innovations and value-added products are essential. Kiva Containers in Phoenix, Arizona, is

one such company developing new strategies to hold on to its customers. The family-owned company was founded in 1957 as a corrugated paper and cardboard packaging manufacturer, but much has changed in the last generation. Kiva is now investing much of its capital into new facilities for the manufacture of corrugated plastic boxes. This more durable product commands a higher price and the higher profit margin Kiva needs to compete in the rough waters of their regional market. This new line also fits Kiva's other strategy: one-stop-shopping. By expanding horizontally and offering a variety of packaging options, Kiva Containers can supply a customer's every need.

Family ownership is still very common and supports the country's thriving work ethic. Rocco Enterprises, Inc., the parent company of Shady Brook Farms, is a great example of how outstanding quality and family ownership can be maintained throughout a company's growth. Rocco began in 1939 in Harrisonburg, Virginia, as a small feed company; today, it employs 4,100 people, and the third generation of the founding family will soon assume its management. Not only has Rocco kept the company in the family, it has developed an extremely successful business: Shady Brook Farms is the number-one brand of fresh turkey products on the East Coast.

Though corporate research labs develop a large quantity of new products, small manufacturing concerns are often on the leading edge of new technologies as well. As in the past, many of them spring from the ideas and insights of a single individual or a small group, and sometimes develop into new products and processes that eventually impact an entire industry. Back in

1899, George Witt, the founder of The Witt Company of Cincinnati, Ohio, patented the corrugated ash can. By incorporating this unique design and using a hot-dip galvanizing process, Witt popularized the ash can, and the company's durable cans earned a reputation as products of the highest quality. This reputation is what helped Witt expand its business. For many years a stable and prosperous company, Witt built on its successes; the company expanded its hot dip galvanizing department to meet the growing number of orders from the construction industry. Today Witt, still family-owned, owns its own galvanizing subsidiary, and — like many small and mid-sized companies — is considered a valuable supplier by larger companies.

There are thousands of specialized niches in the economy that are filled by small manufacturers' products. Una-Dyn is one such supplier, and its products have been instrumental to the development of the plastics industry. Established in 1957 for the manufacture of air drying equipment, Universal Dynamics encountered an opportunity to supply dry air to DuPont for their nylon producing process. The company's continuing experience supplying dry air to the plastics industry was crucial to the development of new, specialized plastics materials. In conjunction with the growing demand for plastics, Una-Dyn's business has grown to include dryers, loaders, blenders and complete materials handling systems for the plastics industry.

That there is strength in diversity could not have a better example than in U.S. industry, where smaller manufacturers are the heart of the world's strongest economy. And the critical contribution small businesses make to the economy is reflected in national employment statistics: they are collectively the country's largest employers. While the larger corporations that a global economy fosters are flagships of the approaching age, the fleet is made up of small and medium-sized manufacturers that provide world-class quality and specialized, cutting-edge products that will always be in demand.

The Greening of Industry

No one questions the importance of a healthy environment to protect the quality of life and life itself. Over the past quarter century, American industry has spent an estimated $1 trillion to revitalize and replenish the environment and to optimize its future prospects. As a result: in the last seven years, American manufacturers have cut toxic emissions by 43 percent; in the 1990s there are 20 percent more trees than in 1970; and there have been significant, measurable improvements in our air, soil and waterways.

Countless companies have found that when they've changed their production processes in order to reduce their environmental impact — often independent of government regulation — their bottom line has gained, as well. 3M, for instance, has eliminated more than 3.1 billion pounds of pollutants while simultaneously saving over $710 million in the process during the past two decades.

Dow Chemical initiated an effort three years ago that is expected to eliminate 56 million pounds of hazardous and non-hazardous waste. While it costs $11 million, the program is expected to trim $12 million in expenses.

U.S. paper and forest companies plant 1 billion seedlings every year — nearly 270,000 a day. As a result, the national supply of trees, which in the 1920s was predicted to last only until 1945, is now increasing —and going into wood construction, daily newspapers, bowling pins, paper towels, insecticides, cleaning compounds, guitars, cereal boxes, foam rubber, furniture, diapers, pencils, lacquer, charcoal and many more products that are a part of daily life.

Companies of all sizes have found that the processes that help reduce waste also reduce the costs of production and result in higher-quality products. Thus, environmental excellence has become a valuable business goal as well as an ethical one. And Americans benefit through an environment that is significantly cleaner than that of 30 years ago.

Healthy trees planted by the forest products industry

Packaging For Consumer Appeal and Environmental Quality

Among the many industries that have met today's environmental challenges with a spirit of innovation is the packaging industry. Over the years, packaging manufacturers have played an integral role in bringing an abundance of consumer goods to the marketplace, developing ways to preserve and protect everything from tomatoes to computers. Today, some of these companies are also in the forefront of waste reduction.

There are many companies that could be cited for their efforts in this area. One good example is Westvaco Corporation, a major manufacturer of paper packaging and specialty chemicals that has excelled in both packaging and environmental achievements. In the mid-1980s, Westvaco introduced cartons that allowed food to be displayed, cooked in either a microwave or conventional oven and served — all in the carton. The product not only cut packaging costs, but reduced packaging material by up to 50 percent compared with conventional cartons made with an outer wrapper and inner tray.

In the 1990s, the company took an important step in waste control by introducing a packaging line with up to 30 percent recovered fiber content, all of it post-consumer. The company has also led in turning wood wastes into useful materials. For instance, it produces an activated carbon that is an essential part of pollution control systems installed in every automobile made in the United States.

The importance of packaging has only grown as a result of the dramatic boom in U.S. exports, with American-made goods shipped across the globe. Packaging industry researchers continue to probe new products that will meet both packaging and environmental needs. "Interactive packages" are being designed that will help maintain the protective environments various products require. Some packages intended to go in the microwave oven are engineered to keep certain foods cold while others cook. Efforts are underway throughout the packaging industry to produce materials of lighter weight or less volume so waste will be reduced at the source. And the edible package — the ultimate in waste reduction — may yet become a reality.

Westvaco packaging

An Orbiting Telescope Eyes the Edge of Space

While new technologies and developments seem to uncover new knowledge every day, the race to create a better future provides tools that may shed some light on the distant past as well. The horrific *Challenger* disaster of 1986 shattered the public's confidence in America's space shuttle program, but the exploration of outer space has continued to make enormous strides. Nothing better illustrates this progress than the completion and installation of the Hubble Space Telescope in the early 1990s. The telescope was designed and manufactured at Hughes Danbury Optical Systems, Inc., and prepared for the mission by Lockheed. Probing the earliest stages of the universe by capturing its most distant transmitted light, which might indicate just how old the universe actually is, the telescope has already imparted highly significant observations.

Almost immediately after the telescope was launched into space, it was discovered that the optical mirror had been incorrectly ground, and the imperfections compromised the instrument's ability to gather and transmit accurate images. Almost as fascinating as the telescope itself was the correction of these imperfections, which required a corrective lens from Perkin-Elmer and repair work in space by a space shuttle crew. The successful repair has allowed the Hubble to probe the farthest corners of the universe and gather clues about our origin and destiny.

Left, optical telescope assembly for the Hubbell Space Telescope in final assembly stand, Danbury, Connecticut, 1984; above, an illustration of the telescope inside and out

Developing Business Cultures Where Learning Never Stops

Education is a very high-priority activity for many manufacturers in the 1990s. As the American economy is increasingly based on knowledge, rather than craft or hand labor, and as the manufacturing arena has become global in scope and fiercely competitive, a new emphasis on training is boosting the success of American businesses. In fact, manufacturers spend more than $35 billion annually on worker training and development.

Educational programs of numerous varieties are helping firms meet some formidable challenges. The rising technological complexity of manufacturing processes has changed the nature of factory work dramatically in many plants and demands a work force with skills in computers, problem-solving and other areas to match the challenges of the new environment.

One major aspect of increased competitiveness is higher productivity, and many companies have found that the way to achieve that is to train workers so that each person can work to his or her full potential. Such efforts increase productivity. In fact, manufacturing productivity increases have far exceeded the service sector.

Operating successfully in the global marketplace demands world-class quality, and again, education is indispensable. Many companies have restructured their operations and their employees' jobs by establishing self-managed work teams. Specialized training is the key to empowering employees, so they can release the full productive potential of technology and their own ability.

Such training efforts have undeniable benefits for the employees involved. At the most basic level, as education helps a business meet the goals of increased productivity, lower costs, higher quality and more effec-

tive organization, it helps that business prosper, thus enhancing future prospects for employees. Increasing skill and competence helps workers succeed in the company and increase their earning power. Developing the ability to perform more complex, responsible and challenging work often leads to greater job satisfaction and self-esteem for workers as well.

Numerous manufacturers exemplify the power of training in today's economy. One of the most dramatic situations occurred at Will-Burt, a small machine parts company in Ohio. In 1985, the company was facing probable liquidation, primarily due to quality problems that had resulted in numerous product liability lawsuits on parts the company had supplied to major customers. Harry Featherstone, the company's new president, was informed by its board of directors that he had only six weeks to turn Will-Burt around and prevent liquidation.

Following some financial arrangements that assured temporary survival, Featherstone insisted on a major investment in education for his workers, whose skills he judged as being short of what was required. All 280 employees were tested in reading and math, and all workers were required to participate in math classes. This initial step was followed by a voluntary course on reading blueprints, which was eventually taken by almost everyone. Featherstone went on to establish an in-house business school that offers a "mini-MBA," an overview of every department in the company and their functions.

The results have been spectacular. As quality soared, earnings followed. Prior to 1985, company earnings had never exceeded $400,000; by 1987, earnings had increased enough to

Students learn basic scientific principles and discover the excitement of technology at the Motorola Museum of Electronics in Schaumburg, Illinois

repay $1 million of the 1985 loan that had helped finance the company's survival.

Employee morale has shown a marked improvement as well. Absenteeism has dropped significantly, the number of employees late to work per week has dropped from a majority of the work force to a tiny fraction and the safety of the work environment has improved immeasurably. Annual employee turnover has dropped from 35 percent in 1986 to 1 percent by 1994.

Among larger manufacturers, Motorola is renowned for its training programs — and for the high quality standards to which those programs have contributed. The company launched what it calls "Motorola University" in 1981 with three people; today the training facility employs 200 full-time educators and another 400 on contract. Motorola spends approximately 4 percent of payroll on

training, and its employees average 40 hours per year on instruction. By the year 2000, the company plans to quadruple the instruction time.

Employees are trained in basic skills of English and math and also take courses in team building and problem solving. In addition to classroom training, the company promotes "embedded learning," which allows new employees to earn regular wages while learning under an experienced worker's guidance.

Ford Motor Company provides still another example. A comprehensive training program that was developed cooperatively between the company and the United Auto Workers has been a major factor in improving Ford's productivity, quality, employee involvement and profitability. Under the Education, Development and Training Program, Ford established seven educational programs called "Avenues for Growth," which offer employees a systematic

approach to lifelong learning. Areas covered range from basic skills to automotive technology to college courses. By mid-1994, more than 78,000 employees had participated in at least one of the options. Along with employee involvement, these training programs were instrumental in propelling the drive for quality, productivity and profits that helped Ford make a dramatic comeback.

These programs are similar to those of many other manufacturers. Firms throughout the country are also working with local schools, colleges and technical institutes to prepare future employees for the modern manufacturing workplace of the twenty-first century. In an era in which government training programs have had disappointing results, America's manufacturers are developing cultures where learning never stops.

Epilogue: American Manufacturing Meets the Global Challenge

I t was only a few years ago that observers of the American economy were talking of "deindustrialization" and mourning the downward slide of the country's manufacturing sector. Many proclaimed the end of America's industrial era, and an inability to compete in an increasingly global marketplace. Even the giants of the economy appeared to be losing ground.

Then, in the 1980s, an amazing comeback got underway. Many American companies looked hard at the competition, listened to their customers and learned their lessons. Industrial innovators all but reinvented their companies, turning to new ideas about management, developing larger roles for employees, sharpening the focus on customers and investing in powerful automation technologies. The wisdom of quality-management experts such as W. Edwards Deming attracted new attention, and many manufacturers implemented total quality management programs.

In industries all over the country, ambitious goals in innovation, productivity and quality were coupled with management methods that put increased power, freedom and authority in the hands of workers at all levels. Education and training became a central focus in many large and small companies, along with incentives that helped people see themselves as stakeholders in their company's success. Manufacturing productivity rose an average of 3.04 percent annually from 1985 to 1994, compared to 0.98 in the non-farm business sector overall. U.S. productivity now stands above that of our global competitors.

Disciplined by a focus on customer demands for quality and low cost in a competitive environment, manufacturers redesigned their inventory practices, and their design and production processes. Product quality rose dramatically. Customized manufacturing began meeting the precise and diverse needs of each customer.

The result of the industrial transformation is a remarkable upsurge in market share of major industries. Especially welcome are dramatic comebacks in three vital industries: automobiles, steel and semiconductors. By 1992, for example, the American semiconductor enterprise had regained its global preeminence in a $77 billion global industry. Automobiles produced in the United States claimed almost 75 percent of the domestic market in 1994, up from just over 70 percent in 1991. From 1985 to 1994, American steel exports quadrupled.

Worldwide dominance in such areas as personal computers and assorted high-tech industries, as well as aerospace, pharmaceuticals and biotechnology, is bolstering the nation's export strength, helping to generate what management expert Peter Drucker called a manufacturing export boom "unprecedented in American history and, indeed, in economic history altogether." Meanwhile, the National Association of Manufacturers has advocated policies that are conducive to U.S. manufacturing competitiveness in a global environment.

Manufacturers' determination to triumph in global competition is matched by a renewed resolve to tackle another huge challenge — government policies that impose unnecessarily high non-production costs and discourage investment, exports and job creation. Members of the NAM have banded together to increase their effectiveness in the policy arena and improve the economic climate for manufacturers.

The association's educational affiliate, The Manufacturing Institute, is pursuing a multi-year effort to take the manufacturing message to Capitol Hill, the White House and federal agencies, the news media and other key audiences. Only a full understanding of manufacturing will enable the nation to adopt long-term public policies that will support a strong manufacturing environment at home.

Will the coming 100 years mark another "American Century?" While no one knows for certain what the future holds nor how to meet the challenges that tomorrow will bring, America's manufacturers are taking the extraordinary steps needed to renew their enterprises, empower their employees and meet customers' needs and global challenges alike. As for the future, the prolific inventor Charles F. Kettering offered some sound advice: "We work day after day after day, not to finish things, but to make the future brighter — because we will spend the rest of our lives there."

Acknowledgments

This book tells the largely untold story of how manufacturing in America has improved the standard of living and the quality of life for our citizens over the past 100 years, while continuing to pave the way for conquering future competitive challenges through innovation and vigor. The story it tells is a testament to the men and women who have been — and continue to be — the key element in U.S. manufacturing's success.

Coinciding with the centennial celebration of the National Association of Manufacturers, the publication of this book reflects the contributions and efforts of many. Foremost, I wish to pay tribute to Dana Mead, chairman and CEO of Tenneco Inc., for his vision and generous support in making this project possible.

Manufacturing in America: A Legacy of Excellence was sponsored by Tenneco Inc. and Case Corporation, with additional support from Ingersoll-Rand Company. Printing was donated by Worzalla Publishing Company on paper donated by Westvaco Corporation. Worzalla also bound the book using cloth donated by Industrial Coatings Group, Inc., and used embossing dies provided by Owasso Graphic Arts. My special thanks to Jean-Pierre Rosso of Case, J. Frank Travis of Ingersoll-Rand, Charles Nason of Worzalla, Rudolph G. Johnstone of Westvaco, Mike Holt, Bob Matts and John Clark of ICG and Jerry Voight of Owasso.

Two NAM employees warrant special recognition. Ladd Biro, senior vice president of marketing for the NAM and Manufacturing Institute president, provided the steady leadership to see this ambitious project through from the concept stage to finished product. This book was his idea, and without his absolute refusal to give up when the going got tough, it never would have been produced.

Doug Kurkul, assistant vice president for member communications for the NAM and the book's executive editor/project director, tirelessly shepherded this book through every stage, from editorial to production to marketing. His suggestions and improvements throughout the eight-month process ensured that we captured the legacy of U.S. manufacturing excellence in this volume.

We are also indebted to the following people for a variety of significant contributions: Stan Burns, Peter Eisenstadt, Kathleen Gruber, Oliver Jensen, Jim Johnson, Tom O'Hanlon, Steve Wheeler, and especially Bronwyn Evans, whose exuberance is reflected in the insightful additions she made to the manuscript.

Particularly helpful were the many NAM member companies, small and large, that provided information on their own firm's historical contributions and milestones. Even a 1,000-page volume could not do justice to their many and varied contributions to our nation and their individual communities.

Many other people contributed to the success of this book. In particular, I would like to thank, for their assistance and efforts, John Castellani, Arthur House, Peg Root, Linda Ambrose and Bob Fagan of Tenneco Inc.; Ellen Robinson, Bill Masterson and Dave Rogers of Case Corporation; Gordon Stables, Dick Johnson and Stanley Parkhill of Ingersoll-Rand Company; Jim Buzzard, Ned Massee and William Fuller III of Westvaco; Dr. Mike Nash, John Williams and Barbara Hall of the Hagley Museum and Library; David Bowes of Oakleaf Associates; Mark Robbins, Scherri Jacobsen and Leon Saffelle of The Manufacturing Institute; and William Morin, Norma Leake, Tonya Frazier, Elaine Toms, Dave Hiergesell, Ted Dubin, Kristin Nelson and Mea Rhee of the NAM.

Last, but most of all, I offer a special thank you to the manufacturers of the United States of America. This book tells your story.

Jerry J. Jasinowski

Chairman, The Manufacturing Institute

October 1995

Throughout the past 100 years, innovative U.S. manufacturers have identified everyday problems and exercised ingenuity to help society address, and sometimes solve, those problems. Likewise, manufacturers' inventions and products have enabled others — in medicine, engineering, the sciences, services, government, universities and so forth — to address still other challenges. The ongoing result is a nation with the highest living standards and both economic and military power that are second to none. Here are some noteworthy developments related to *Manufacturing in America*.

1895

- On January 22, the National Association of Manufacturers is founded in Cincinnati, Ohio
- King C. Gillette invents the safety razor with disposable blades
- The nation's first large hydroelectric power plant, built by Westinghouse, is completed at Niagara Falls
- The Reliance Building, an early skyscraper, is built in Chicago
- W. K. Kellogg processes the first flaked cereal
- The Postum Cereal Company is formed by C. W. Post
- The first patent for an automobile powered by a gasoline engine is issued to George B. Seldon
- The following companies are founded: Acme-Cleveland Corporation, Allegheny International Corporation, Archbold Industries, Lever Bros. Co., Lincoln Electric Co., National Starch & Chemical Company, OshKosh B'Gosh, Inc., Robinson Industries, Inc., Stora Newton Falls, Toledo-Commutator, United Aluminum Corporation, Vaughn-Bassett Furniture Co., York Wallcoverings, among others

1896

- Duryea brothers begin production and sale of gasoline-powered cars
- William Ramsay discovers helium
- Ernest Rutherford discovers magnetic detection of electrical waves
- First successful model of diesel locomotive engine introduced by Ingersoll-Rand Company
- George Washington Carver joins Tuskegee Institute where he continues his landmark research in plant growth and agriculture

R.R. Donnelly and Sons Co.'s first bookplate, 1897

1897

- Francis and Freelan Stanley introduce the first commercially successful car powered by a steam engine, the Stanley Steamer
- Charles Parsons' invention of the first practical steam turbogenerator sets the stage for the *Turbinia* to set sail, sparking the age of ocean liners
- E&T Fairbanks Company holds 113 patents for improvements and inventions in measuring weight
- First demonstration of the cathode ray tube, which eventually leads to the development of television
- First major use of paperboard boxes by National Biscuit Company
- Postum Cereal Company introduces Grape Nuts cereal
- Campbell Soup markets tomato soup, the first of its condensed soup line
- Malaria bacillus discovered by Ronald Ross
- J. J. Thomson discovers the electron

1898

- Robinson Danforth enters food market with Purina Wheat and a line of whole-wheat breakfast cereals; would become known as Ralston Purina Company
- First U.S. subway system opens in Boston
- Superior Technical Ceramics, St. Albans, Vermont, is founded
- First magnetic recording of sound
- Western Cartridge Company, later a key part of Olin Corporation, constructs its first plant in East Alton, Illinois
- The semi-automatic glass-forming machine is developed by F. C. Ball; the first step at mechanizing the manufacture of glass jars
- Frank and Charles Seiberling establish the Goodyear Tire & Rubber Co., which becomes the nation's largest tire maker by 1917
- William Ramsay discovers the inert atmospheric gases xenon, krypton and neon
- First photos taken utilizing artificial light

1899

- Henry Timken establishes The Timken Roller Bearing Axle Company in St. Louis; moves to Canton, Ohio, in 1902; Mr. Timken would become instrumental in several advancements, including the conversion to tapered roller bearings in railroad freight cars
- Kellogg's Corn Flakes first sold (under the name Sanitas)
- George Witt, founder of The Witt Company, patents the first corrugated ash (garbage) can
- The Heisler-geared locomotive hauls lumber and minerals
- W. W. Sly conceives, patents and begins the manufacture of the first screen-type of dust collectors made in the U.S.; company now called Sly Inc.
- Chase Manhattan Bank is founded

1900

- George Eastman manufactures the first Brownie camera with roll film

- The first Browning revolvers are manufactured

- F. E. Myers Co. in Ashland, Ohio, now part of Pentair Corp., builds its first fully automatic electric pump

- Abbott Alkaloidal Company is incorporated; is renamed Abbott Laboratories in 1910

1901

- Monsanto is founded, producing saccharin, caffeine and vanillin, the earliest of the firm's many products

- The century of electricity begins, following the century of steam

- J. P. Morgan organizes U.S. Steel Corporation, now USX Corporation

- President Theodore Roosevelt, in conjunction with manufacturers, pursues a major improvement in U.S. naval capabilities

- The hormone adrenaline is first isolated

Harley-Davidson motorcycle, early 1900s

1902

- Clarence Spicer founds Spicer Manufacturing Company, today's Dana Corp. of Toledo, Ohio

- "The Famous Ever-Ready Electric Lights" make their commercial debut at the first Electrical Show at Madison Square Garden

- Standard Oil first substitutes Bayonne Steel barrels for wooden barrels

1903

- Henry Ford, with capital of $100,000, founds the Ford Motor Company

- The Wright brothers, Wilbur and Orville, pilot the first manned flights in the *Flyer 1*

- Harley-Davidson manufactures its first motorcycle

- J. P. Morgan founds the International Mercantile Marine Company

- First coast-to-coast crossing of North America by car: 65 days

- Willis Carrier installs the first building air conditioner in the Sackett-Wilhelms Lithographing and Publishing Company in Brooklyn, New York

- R. A. Zsigmondy invents the ultramicroscope

- Richard Steiff designs the first teddy bears

- Union Oil, later Unocal Corporation, builds the first oil tanker in the world

1904

- Benjamin Holt invents crawler track to replace tractor wheels; his company later merges with C. L. Best Tractor Co. and is renamed Caterpillar, Inc.

- First railroad tunnel is built under Hudson River between Manhattan and New Jersey

- William C. Gorgas eradicates Yellow Fever

- Goodyear makes first detachable rim, which enables fast car tire change

- The first ultraviolet lamp is introduced

- F. S. Kipping discovers silicones

- F. M. Becket of the U.S. is one of several who share in the initial development of stainless steel, a combination of chromium and steel that does not rust

Ingersoll-Rand's diesel locomotive, right, 1896

Rambler chassis assembly, 1902

1905

- A new medicinal product named Vick's Magic Croup Salve is introduced; later called Vick's Vaporub

- Special Theory of Relativity formulated by Albert Einstein

- Rayon yarn is manufactured commercially through viscose process

- The first neon light signs appear

Lackawanna Iron & Steel Company, 1908

1906

- Paper milk cartons are made for the first time by G.W. Maxwell in San Francisco

- The Automatic Machinery and Tool Company introduces the first true jukebox

- American Greetings Corporation of Cleveland, Ohio, is founded

- Kellogg Company is organized as the Battle Creek Toasted Corn Flake Company

- Reginald A. Fessenden broadcasts the first long-distance voice transmission on Christmas Eve

- Multiplex Company of Ballwin, Missouri, is founded as the Multiplex Faucet Company

- Novocain anesthetic is introduced

1907

- Leo Baekeland invents first thermoplastic: Bakelite

- Lee De Forest patents the triode vacuum tube

- American pathologist Ross Harrison develops tissue culture techniques

- The War Department procures its first plane; the contractor — the Wright brothers

- Frank S. Washburn founds the American Cyanamid Company

- Pittsburgh Reduction Company becomes the Aluminum Company of America (Alcoa)

- The Pharmaceutical Research and Manufacturers of America is founded under the name of American Association of Pharmaceutical Chemists

- Bell Labs has its unofficial beginnings in the combined research departments of Western Electric and AT&T

- Domino Sugar Corp. marks its centennial

1908

- General Motors Corporation formed

- Henry Ford introduces the Model T

- General Electric's Dr. William D. Coolidge renders tungsten ductile, paving the way for modern incandescent lighting

- A steel-toothed drill bit used for drilling oil wells is invented

- Murray Spengler, who later co-founds the Hoover Company, patents the electric vacuum

- The American Institute of Chemical Engineers is founded

1909

- The outboard motor, designed by Ole Evinrude, is introduced; it quickly replaces steam and foot-driven motors for boats and spurs a new industry

- The electrocardiograph is invented, using electricity to bring new diagnostic capabilities to the practice of medicine

- Briggs & Stratton begins manufacturing small, gasoline-powered engines

- The Construction Industry Manufacturing Association holds the first major U.S. exhibit of construction machines

- The first wireless message is sent from New York to Chicago

Elmer Sperry, left, experimenting with his gyroscope

1910

- Alcoa introduces aluminum foil
- Schmidt and Osius join with Hamilton Beach Manufacturing Company to sell their electric egg beater
- Elmer Sperry invents the gyrocompass and establishes the Sperry Gyroscope Company
- Hallmark Cards Inc. of Kansas City, Missouri, begins operations
- Lukens Steel of Coatesville, Pennsylvania, celebrates its centennial

1911

- Maytag produces its first electric washing machine
- The J. I. Case Company begins producing automobiles as the Case Motor Works
- Frederick Taylor publishes his first book on scientific management
- Joseph Eaton and Viggio Torbensen file for incorporation as the Torbensen Gear and Axle Company, later to be renamed the Eaton Corporation
- Standard Oil is broken up into 33 separate companies under the Sherman Antitrust Act, just as gasoline sales surge due to the growing popularity of the automobile
- The forerunner of Whirlpool Corporation, Upton Machine Co., is started in Michigan
- Campbell's Soup becomes one of the first nationally marketed food products
- The first Indianapolis 500 is won by Ray Harroun with an average speed of 74 mph

1912

- Charles F. Kettering develops the electrical system for automobiles including an electric ignition or "self-starter"
- Packard builds the first truck to cross the continent under its own power
- Cadillac receives the coveted Dewar Trophy for introducing the first car with an electric self-starter, electric lighting and ignition
- Marmon introduces the rear view mirror for automobiles
- General Electric introduces the first electric toaster
- A process for manufacturing cellophane is invented by Edwin Bradenberger
- F. W. Woolworth Company is founded
- G. H. Strayer organizes the Erie Steel Construction Company as a structural steel fabrication and erection firm
- The first successful parachute jump is made

1913

- Henry Ford applies a moving assembly line to the manufacture of cars, making automobiles universally affordable
- ESCO, the Electric Steel Foundry Company, today a world leader in steel technology, is founded in Portland, Oregon
- Aluminum foil is used for the first time in food packaging, including Life Savers candies
- Igor Sikorsky designs and flies the first multi-motor plane
- Thermal cracking oil refining process developed by Robert E. Humphreys and W. M. Burton of Standard Oil Company
- Ernst Alexanderson of General Electric Company invents a greatly improved radio transmitter
- H. Geiger introduces the first successful electrical device which counts individual alpha rays and is called the Geiger counter
- Zippers, although in use since 1891, become popular

1914

- Members of President Wilson's cabinet unsuccessfully advocate Post Office Department ownership of telephone and telegraph service
- The first practical photography color process, Autochrome, is invented by Alpheus Hyatt Verrill
- The Elgin Sweeper Company sells its first street sweeper
- The first traffic lights — red and green lights only — appear in Cleveland, Ohio
- Studebaker provides the first automobile gas gauge that is located on the dashboard
- The U.S. completes construction of the Panama Canal, making shipment of manufactured goods faster

Dodge assembly, 1914-1920

An Elgin Sweeper model, 1914

1915

- Giddings & Lewis Inc. of Fond Du Lac, Wisconsin, begins manufacture of horizontal boring drills and milling machines; the firm was founded in 1859

- World War I leads to a chronic steel shortage, prompting Timken to enter the steel business

- Albert Einstein postulates his General Theory of Relativity

- Henry Ford develops a farm tractor

- First transcontinental phone call is made between Alexander Graham Bell in New York and Dr. Thomas A. Watson in San Francisco

- Wireless service is established between U.S. and Japan

- Ford produces its one millionth car

- Motorized taxicabs appear on streets

- Corning Glass Works introduces Pyrex heat-resistant glass, used primarily for bakeware

- Maytag introduces the first gas-powered washer, the Multi-Motor, targeted for homes located in areas where electricity is not yet available

- Sonar is invented

- The Donaldson Company, Inc. of Minneapolis is founded

1916

- A new antiseptic, Dakin's Fluid, is invented by Dr. Henry D. Dakin

- Heparin, an important advance in the prevention of blood clotting, is discovered

- William E. Boeing flies his first plane, the B&W Model 1, and forms The Boeing Company

- Kelvinator develops an electrical refrigeration unit

- Ed Halliburton begins a career in the oil industry

Eveready Radio Battery advertisement

1917

- U.S. involvement in World War I requires mobilization and product line changes at many factories

- World's largest reflecting Hooker telescope (100-inches) is installed at Mount Wilson, California

- 300,000 trucks are built for the armed forces in World War I

- Taylor-Wharton Iron & Steel Company celebrates its 175th anniversary

1918

- World War I ends

- The Automatic Hook and Eye Company improves the design of the zipper and acquires a contract with the U.S. Navy for 10,000 zip-fasteners for uniforms

- Regular airmail service is established between New York City and Washington, D.C.

- Hertz begins car rental business

- Kelvinator markets the first successful mechanical refrigerator for home use

- American astronomer Harlow Shapley discovers the true dimensions of the Milky Way

1919

- Radio Corporation of America (RCA) is founded

- Joseph Johnson and William Seidemann invent interchangeable socket wrenches — they later form Snap-on Tools Corporation

- Maytag introduces the first electric washing machine with an aluminum tub

- The American Farm Bureau is founded

- First experiments with and introduction of short-wave radio take place

- Nebraska Consolidated Mills, now known as ConAgra, Inc. is founded

Electric motor manufacturing at Emerson Electric, circa 1921

1920

- Crown Cork & Seal Company, Inc. unveils "Dixie," the automatic filler which revolutionizes the soft drink industry
- Westinghouse Company opens the first American broadcasting station, Pittsburgh's KDKA; overnight commercial broadcasting emerges
- Westinghouse introduces its Aeriola receivers, RCA its Radiola Superheterodyne
- First airmail flight from New York to San Francisco
- Hermann Staudinger shows that small molecules polymerize (form long chains of molecules) by chemical interaction
- Eveready capitalizes on broadcasting boom with a line of Eveready radio batteries; sales of flashlight batteries reach 50 million
- The world's first postage meter is introduced to speed mailroom operations
- The first hand-held hair dryers are introduced by the American Racine Universal Motor Company
- John T. Thompson invents the "tommy" submachine gun
- Eddie Bauer's Tennis Shop opens in Seattle, beginning the 75-year legacy of Eddie Bauer, Inc.
- Duesenberg, maker of fine automobiles, introduces four-wheel hydraulic brakes

1921

- First radio broadcast of a baseball game is made from Polo Grounds in New York City
- Omaha, Nebraska, telephone system offers local telephone dialing service
- Johnson & Johnson sells the first Band-Aids
- The American Institute of Steel Construction is founded

Eli Lilly pharmaceutical production

1922

- John Harwood invents the self-winding wristwatch (patented in 1924)
- Insulin is first administered to diabetic patients
- Dr. Alexis Carrel of the Rockefeller Institute announces his discovery of leukocytes, or white corpuscles, as the agents in the blood that prevent the spread of infection
- Kohler Co. introduces the Automatic Power and Light generator which brings portable power to the job site

1923

- Lee De Forest demonstrates a process for sound motion pictures
- Colonel Jacob Schick patents the electric razor
- John B. Tytus invents continuous hot-strip rolling of steel
- Charles F. Jordan makes the first public demonstration of a television system; viewers see the silhouette of a hand waving
- RCA's Vladimir K. Zworykin, the "father of television," makes the first demonstration of the all-electronic television camera tube
- T. W. Miller, Sr., founder of Faultless Rubber, files specifications for a one-piece golf ball compounded of rubber, zinc oxide, sulfur and glue
- The photoelectric cell is developed, converting light into electricity and setting events in motion towards the eventual harnessing of solar power
- The LaPlant Choate Manufacturing Company produces bulldozers on a large scale
- The first antiknock gasoline is marketed in the U.S.
- Rhyne Lumber Company of Newport, Tennessee, is founded
- The J. I. Case Company introduces its Prairie Combine in Kansas
- The first transatlantic phone call is made via short-wave radio

1924

- Ford Motor Company produces its 10 millionth Model T
- Man-made insecticides used for the first time
- U.S. becomes leading producer of coal and steel
- 2.5 million radios in use in the U.S.
- The first transatlantic photographs, a precursor to television, are sent to the U.S. from England
- The first self-contained electric refrigerator is introduced
- Clarence Birdseye invents a successful process for freezing food without dehydrating it or losing its flavor
- The Chlorine Institute, which is dedicated to maintaining correct levels of disinfection throughout the drinking water supply, is founded

Kohler Company bathtub manufacturing, late 1920s

1925

- Walter P. Chrysler founds the Chrysler Corporation
- The first electrically produced disc is released by the Victor Talking Machine Co.
- 3M introduces masking tape
- Bell Labs is incorporated as a subsidiary of AT&T and Western Electric

1926

- The first liquid fuel rocket is fired by Robert H. Goddard in Auburn, Massachusetts
- A new electric recording technique is developed called the "Electrola"
- Eastman Kodak produces the first 16mm movie film
- Cushioned cork-centered baseballs are introduced
- Buick introduces the foot-controlled dimmer switch
- Vinyl becomes one of the most common plastics
- The first motion picture with sound, *Don Juan*, is released
- The National Broadcasting Company (NBC) is incorporated
- Waldo Semon at B. F. Goodrich discovers polyvinyl chloride (PVC)
- The H. J. Heinz Company registers the keystone image on ketchup labels as its trademark

1927

- Charles A. Lindbergh flies his monoplane, *Spirit of St. Louis*, solo nonstop from New York to Paris in 33.5 hours
- Airplanes first used to "dust" crops with insecticide
- Warner Brothers produces the sound film, *The Jazz Singer*, commencing America's love affair with movies
- Continental Bakery's Wonder Bread and Hostess Cakes rise in popularity
- First transatlantic phone call made via radio
- Stone Container Corporation is established as a major supplier of packaging
- Cellophane is perfected by DuPont
- Taylor Machine Works, Louisville, Mississippi, is founded
- Ford Motor company discontinues the Model T after 15 million have been sold
- Marriott opens its first drive-up restaurant and A&W Root Beer stand in Washington, D.C.
- Harold Black invents the negative feedback amplifier which reduces distortion and greatly improves telecommunications

1928

- PPG Industries introduces Duplate safety glass for automobiles
- The Galvin Manufacturing Company is founded; name changed to Motorola in 1947
- Philo Farnsworth demonstrates the world's first all-electronic television in California for Crocker Research Labs
- Warner Brothers produces the first feature-length complete talkie, *Lights of New York*
- First color motion pictures are exhibited by George Eastman in Rochester, New York
- First scheduled television broadcasts are made by WGY
- Amelia Earhart becomes the first woman to fly across the Atlantic
- General Mills is incorporated
- Daniel Gerber creates the first strained baby food product
- The La-Z-Boy Chair Company is founded in Monroe, Michigan
- Eastman Kodak introduces Kodacolor film
- Ford introduces the Model A

1929

- The U.S. becomes the leading nation worldwide in industrial production
- Lt. James Doolittle pilots airplane using instruments alone, including takeoff and landing
- Bell Labs experiments with color TV
- American manufacturers begin to make aluminum furniture (especially chairs)
- Eastman Kodak introduces 16mm color movie film
- Dr. Edwin H. Land develops Polaroid glasses
- Outboard Marine Corporation is established
- 7-Up is introduced under name "Lithiated Lemon"
- Bausch & Lomb manufactures Ray-Ban sunglasses for Army Air Corps; markets to the public in 1936
- Frigidaire produces its one millionth refrigerator and also introduces the first chest-type freezer for the home
- Postum purchases General Foods and becomes General Foods Corporation
- W. A. Morrison introduces quartz-crystal clocks for precise timekeeping

Cellophane development at DuPont, Dr. Hale Charch

Continental Baking advertisement, 1925

1930

- The Great Depression hits full force
- Large-scale electro-mechanical analog computer is built by U.S. scientist Vannevar Bush
- The first Toastmaster toaster is introduced by McGraw-Electric
- The first true supermarket opens in Jamaica, New York
- 3M begins making Scotch brand cellophane tape
- Wrought iron is developed by James Aston and used by A. M. Byers Co.
- Sunbeam Corporation introduces the Mixmaster electric mixer
- Elmer Sperry develops the first successful automatic pilot
- Mead incorporates as the Mead Corporation
- Van Rooy Coffee Co. begins operations in Cleveland, Ohio
- Continental Baking Company introduces sliced bread and Twinkies
- Photoflash bulbs come into use
- 13.7 million American homes have radios

1931

- Miles Laboratories markets Alka-Seltzer
- Clyde Pangborn and Hugh Herndon fly nonstop from Sabishiro, Japan, to Wenatchee, Washington, in 41 hours
- Spicer-Dufay process of natural color photography is introduced
- Beech Nut introduces its strained baby food
- Freon, which is later used for refrigeration, is developed
- Monroe Auto Equipment Company develops first successful direct-acting shock absorber
- Walker Manufacturing Company patents the louvered-tube muffler construction

Eveready advertisement for flashlights and batteries

1932

- Edwin Land invents a synthetic light polarizer
- Balloon tires are produced for farm tractors
- Carlton Magee of Oklahoma City invents the parking meter
- The first diesel-electric train is introduced by Ingersoll-Rand
- Construction of the Golden Gate Bridge begins

1933

- Clifford B. Hannay of Westerlo, New York, designs a mechanism to be used as a storage and delivery device for hose; called Hannay Reels, today the firm produces thousands of hose and cable reels each month
- Vladimir K. Zworykin, director of electronics for RCA, adds iconoscope to TV; high-quality television is almost complete, but early sets cost as much as a car
- Great Lakes Chemical Corporation of West Lafayette, Indiana, is established
- The Industrial Safety Equipment Association is founded
- In response to the depression, Lincoln Electric Co. creates a pioneering incentive bonus system to reward workers for making the company more profitable, a program that is still in effect today

1934

- IBM introduces the first popular electric typewriter, the Electromatic
- The Zephyr, a stainless steel train, makes its first trip, from Denver to Chicago, setting a speed record of 112 miles per hour
- A refrigeration process for meat cargoes is devised
- Rubbermaid introduces the first rubber dustpan
- Percy Shaw invents cat's-eye road studs
- First electron microscope is developed

Manufacturers advertise at ballparks, here League Park in Cleveland

1935

- First nighttime major league baseball game is played under G.E. lights in Cincinnati, Ohio
- Robert Watson Watt builds radar equipment to detect aircraft
- John L. Lewis organizes the CIO (Congress of Industrial Organization)
- Polyethylene, a lightweight non-toxic plastic is created
- Plexiglas, a crystal-clear plastic used for furniture, jewelry, clocks, aircraft windows, taillights, boat windshields, camera lenses and more, is introduced
- Eastman Kodak invents Kodachrome color film

Soap manufacturing at The Proctor & Gamble Company, Cincinatti, OH, 1930s

1936

- Douglas' DC-3 begins passenger service
- The completion of the Boulder Dam makes possible the first transmission of electricity from Arizona to Los Angeles
- Dirigible *Hindenburg* lands at Lakehurst, New Jersey, after transatlantic flight
- Ford Foundation is established
- Henry Luce begins publication of *Life* magazine
- Harold and Ruth Swanson begin baking rolls and cakes in their home; they would introduce Archway Home Style Cookies five years later

1937

- The klystron, the heart of the CAT scanner, is invented by Russell and Sigurd Varian, founders of Varian Associates of Palo Alto, California
- For the first time a mine in North America is air-conditioned by refrigeration shafts 3,600 feet underground
- The Ensign-Bickford Company celebrates its centennial, highlighting the introduction of its promising new detonating cord, Primacord
- Eugene Houdry's revolutionary catalytic cracking oil refining process works successfully at a Sun Oil Company refinery
- Hartley Co., Inc., of Columbus, Ohio, is founded
- Insulin is first used to control diabetes
- Crystalline vitamin A and vitamin K concentrates are first obtained
- First transcontinental radio broadcast describes disaster of the *Hindenburg* at Lakehurst

Hannay Reels' office and shop, 1937

1938

- DuPont invents Teflon
- Owens-Illinois and Corning Glass invent fiberglass
- Congress passes the Wagner-O'Day Act which leads to the establishment of the National Industries for the Blind
- Hewlett-Packard sells first product (audio oscillator) to Walt Disney Studios, which creates the animated feature film, *Fantasia*
- Traulsen & Co. of Fort Worth, Texas, begins manufacturing its first fixtures for bakery retailers
- The eight-hour work day and minimum wage become part of basic workplace law
- Wallace Corothers creates nylon at DuPont
- Chester F. Carlson invents the process of xerography; Haliod Co. (today's Xerox Corporation) acquires his license in 1947

1939

- Rocco, Inc., is founded as Rocco Feeds Inc., a small poultry and feed company which grows into the third-largest turkey producer in the U.S.
- The Federal Seed Act establishes the federal practice of mandating product label information
- George Stiblitz of Bell Labs develops a modern digital computer
- *The Wizard of Oz* dramatizes Hollywood's switch from black and white to Technicolor
- Pan-American Airways begins regularly scheduled commercial flights between the U.S. and Europe on the *Dixie Clipper*
- FM (Frequency Modulation) radio is invented by Edwin H. Armstrong
- RCA reaches an agreement with Philo Farnsworth over certain television parts for which Farnsworth had patents; improved television broadcasting began immediately
- Scientists succeed in splitting uranium atoms
- Publicly funded projects constitute two-thirds of construction, up from one-third a decade earlier, before the New Deal
- Butler Manufacturing Company of Kansas City, Missouri, acquires a plant in Galesburg, Illinois, for the purpose of manufacturing grain bins as part of the government's Ever Normal Granary program
- General Motors builds first the diesel-electric freight locomotive
- Peter Drucker authors his first book on business

1940

- Air Products and Chemicals Inc. of Allentown, Pennsylvania, begins operations

- The NAM establishes a National Defense and Mobilization Committee

- First electron microscope demonstrated by RCA

- Sikorsky's VS-300 helicopter, built and tested in 1939, flies successfully

- The cavity magnetron is invented

- 30 million homes in the U.S. have radios

- British-American research program develops the Microwave Early Warning system used in the D-day invasion of France

- Nylon stockings become available nationwide

- Danco Metal Products Inc., of Westlake, Ohio, is founded

1941

- The NAM begins "Preparedness Through Production" campaign

- The portable military bridge is invented by Donald Bailey

- Edwin McMillan and Glenn T. Seaborg discover plutonium (atomic number 94), the key element in the nuclear bomb

- General Mills Company markets Cheerios cereal

- Reedrill, Inc. is founded

- Pitt-Des Moines, Inc. begins operating a shipyard on Neville Island near Pittsburgh, Pennsylvania, to build advanced based sectional docks for the Navy

- Modern windpower is born at Grandpa's Knob, Vermont, when the largest wind turbine is built and delivers 1,250 kilowatts to consumers

- The U.S. enters World War II and marshals previously inconceivable manufacturing might to fight the war

1942

- Wartime needs require an unprecedented industrial mobilization with massive changes in product lines; U.S. aircraft industry produces 86,000 planes during the year

- At the University of Chicago, the first controlled nuclear chain reaction is created by Enrico Fermi as part of the Manhattan Project, the U.S. effort to produce an atomic bomb

- Magnetic recording tape is invented

- A. C. Hartley invents device for clearing fog from airfields

- Henry J. Kaiser develops techniques for building Liberty ships; one of the 10,000-ton ships is completed in eight days

- First electronic digital computer constructed at Iowa State University by Prof. John Atanasoff and Clifford Berry

- Manufacture of construction equipment hits a new high, with virtually all of it going to the U.S. Army and Navy

- The nation's first jet plane, Bell Aircraft Company's XP-59 Aircomet, makes its maiden flight

1943

- Pfizer Inc. successfully mass-produces penicillin

- Bethlehem Steel completes 380 ships for the year and repairs 7,000 more

- 1,300-mile-long "Big Inch" oil pipeline, from Texas to Pennsylvania, begins operation

- Continuous casting in steel manufacturing is introduced

- Two million people are employed in the U.S. aircraft industry

- Selman Waksman discovers streptomycin for the treatment of tuberculosis

- The Stanley Works celebrates its centennial

1944

- Nalco Chemical Company begins its wartime effort producing catalysts needed in the production of high-octane aviation gasoline

- The Steel Shipping Container Institute is founded

- Tennessee Gas and Transmission Company (later Tenneco) completes a natural gas pipeline from Agua Dulce, Texas, to Charleston, West Virginia

- The early computer, the Harvard Mark I, is designed by Howard Aiken

- The 1944 GI Bill begins to put millions of vets through college, upgrading lives and Americans' skill base

- An NAM trade conference in Rye, New York, draws participants from 52 countries

Vladimir Zworykin and RCA's electron microscope, early 1940s

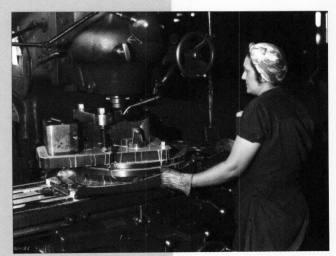

Lukens Steel Company, 1944

1945

- First truly electronic computer built at University of Pennsylvania

- First atomic bomb is tested at Alamogordo, New Mexico, on July 16

- Sun Company's catalytic cracking refinery produces more than 1.1 million barrels of 100-octane gasoline each month

- World War II ends and manufacturers begin to reconvert from wartime production to market-driven manufacturing

- U.S. synthetic rubber production reaches 820,000 tons — up from 8,000 tons in 1941 — thanks to years of rubber industry research in meeting a critical wartime need

Kohler engine assembly, late 1940s

1946

- The Electronic Numerical Integrator and Computer (ENIAC), is designed at the Moore School of Electrical Engineering at the University of Pennsylvania

- John von Neumann at the Institute for Advanced Study, Princeton, New Jersey, designs a computer that stores information and uses binary numbers

- The technique of carbon dating is introduced

- The Atomic Energy Commission is established

- Lakewood Manufacturing of Westlake, Ohio, is founded

1947

- A Bell Labs team led by William Shockley, John Bardeen and Walter Brattain invent the point contact transistor, for which they receive the Nobel Prize

- Bell Aircraft's rocket-powered X-1, piloted by Capt. Charles "Chuck" Yeager, is the first plane to fly at supersonic speed

- Eveready introduces batteries for hearing-aid applications

- International commerce facilitated by General Agreement on Tariffs and Trade (GATT)

- Abbott introduces penicillin in form of tablets

- Reynolds Metals Company markets Reynolds Wrap aluminum foil

- B. F. Goodrich's Frank Herzegh creates tubeless tire

- Dr. Edwin H. Land, founder of Polaroid, invents a process of instant photography

1948

- AMP Inc. introduces the first crimp-applied electrical terminals in strip form, rather than individual pieces, for application by semi-automatic machines

- First plastic, long-playing record is marketed in the U.S., invented by Peter Goldmark

- Rocket missiles reach 78 mile altitude and 3,000 miles per hour in U.S. tests

- A 200-inch reflecting telescope is the now the world's largest in Mount Palomar, California

1949

- Cortisone is discovered by Philip Hench

- U.S. Air Force jet flies across U.S. in 3 hours, 46 minutes

- New antibiotics introduced: Terramycin from Pfizer, Aureomycin from Lederle and Chloromycetin from Parke-Davis

- Haloid Company markets first electrophotographic Model A copier; later becomes Xerox Corporation

- Jervis B. Webb Company of Farmington Hills, Michigan, introduces its electronically coordinated conveyor system

Varian Associates' worker researching thin film sputtering systems

1950

- Varian Associates makes the first high-resolution nuclear magnetic resonance spectrometer for molecular structure research

- Father Gregory Keller, aided by mechanics at Bob's Candies, Inc., of Albany, Georgia, invents a machine to cut and twist candy canes uniformly

- Antihistamines become a popular remedy for colds and allergies

- 1.5 million TV sets in the U.S. (one year later there were approximately 15 million)

- Jack-In-The-Box opens the first fast food restaurant; McDonald's and Burger King follow in 1954

- The first mass-produced computer for business use, UNIVAC 1 (*uni*versal *a*utomatic *c*omputer), is built by the Eckert-Mauchly Computer Corporation

- Businessman Frank McNamara launches the Diners Club card

- The Niagara Mohawk Power Corporation, with roots dating back to 1823, is founded by consolidating three of its operating subsidiaries

- The Levi Strauss & Company, which got its start by making work pants from tent canvas for prospectors during the California gold rush, celebrates its centennial

- Herman Miller, Inc., adopts the Scanlon plan, an employee participation plan

DeSoto assembly line

1951

- During the Korean War, Hotpoint temporarily halts manufacturing refrigerators at its Illinois plant in order to produce jet engines

- Transistor is manufactured commercially by Western Electric

- The first experimental electric power derived from atomic energy is generated at Arco, Idaho

- Approximately 400,000 pounds of penicillin and 350,000 pounds of streptomycin are produced in the U.S. during the year

- Syntex scientists discover norethindrone, the first orally active contraceptive

1952

- Sandmeyer Steel Company of Philadelphia, Pennsylvania, is founded

- First hydrogen bomb exploded at Eniwetok Atoll

- Sony introduces pocket-size radio using transistors

- Contraceptive pill of phosphorated hesperidin is produced

- The NAM's 15-minute television show, *Industry On Parade*, is telecast in 76 of the 78 U.S. television markets

Sandmeyer Steel Company, 1954

1953

- IBM introduces its first commercial computer, the 701

- Dow Chemical Company creates Saran Wrap

- Dynapac, a subsidiary of Svedala International, patents the "ball-and-race principle" for generating vibrations; this was the foundation for today's high volume production of heavy vibratory rollers for compaction and paving

- Raytheon Manufacturing Company introduces the first high-frequency dielectric heating apparatus, now universally known as the microwave

- The Air-Conditioning and Refrigeration Institute is founded

- Cosmic ray observatory erected on Mount Wrangell, Alaska

- A rocket-powered U.S. plane is flown at more than 1,600 mph

1954

- U.S. submarine *Nautilus* converted to nuclear power by General Dynamics' Electric Boat

- Schoolchildren in Pittsburgh, Pennsylvania, are inoculated with an anti-polio serum developed by Dr. Jonas E. Salk

- 29 million U.S. homes have televisions

- Federal Paper Board Company, Inc., becomes listed on the NYSE

- The U.S. contains 6 percent of the world's population but has 60 percent of all cars, 58 percent of all telephones, 45 percent of all radio sets and 34 percent of all railroads

- Charles H. Townes develops masers, which amplify electromagnetic waves for use in radio telescopes

- Swanson introduces frozen TV dinners

- Bell Labs develops the photovoltaic cell which converts sunlight to electricity

- Alcan Aluminum Corporation begins operations

- Regulation of nuclear power is put in the hands of the Atomic Energy Commission

- The first broadcasts of color television begin

- First successful organ transplant, of a kidney, carried out at Harvard Medical School

1955

- Massachusetts Institute of Technology produces ultra high frequency waves

- The U.S. uses its first atomically generated power

- AMP Inc. unveils a fully automatic lead maker that applies electrical terminals to both ends of a cable

- Dr. Jonas E. Salk successfully tests his killed-virus vaccine for poliomyelitis

- IBM launches its 752 computer

- Worthington Industries, Inc., is founded in Columbus, Ohio

1956

- A. Y. McDonald Manufacturing Company of Dubuque, Iowa, celebrates its centennial

- FORTRAN, a logical and algebraic language for programming computers, is developed by John Backus at IBM

- AT&T lays the first transatlantic undersea telephone cables

- Brunswick Corporation installs its first automatic pinsetter

- Albert Sabin develops an oral live-virus vaccine against polio

- General Electric begins producing industrial diamonds

- Los Alamos Laboratory discovers the neutrino, an atomic particle with no electric charge

- Federal-Aid Highway Act passed

1957

- The first satellites, *Sputnik I* and II, are launched by the USSR

- Eveready produces "AA" size alkaline batteries for use in "personal transistor radios"

- Conklin Instrument Corporation of Pleasant Valley, New York, is founded

- Physician Basil Hirschowitz and physicists Curtis and Peters develop the first flexible fiber-optic endoscope

- The J. I. Case Company introduces the first 320 loader/backhoe

- Kiva Container Corp., Phoenix, Arizona, is founded

- The first nuclear electric power plant goes into operation in Shippingport, Pennsylvania

1958

- Convair's Atlas, the first U.S. ICBM missile, is launched and travels 6,300 miles

- The first practical stereo records are marketed

- U.S. satellite, *Explorer I* launches from Cape Canaveral

- NASA is established by the U.S. for the scientific exploration of space

- U.S. launches first moon rocket 79,000 miles from earth, but it fails to reach moon

- Hula hoops, made of polyethylene, are introduced

- Daisy Manufacturing Company produces the first air rifle in Rogers, Arkansas

- Pan Am inaugurates commercial jet service with flight from New York to Paris

- Snorkel Fire Equipment Company is founded to market elevating platforms used for fire fighting and rescue work; company now called Snorkel Economy

- Bank of America introduces BankAmericard, the precursor to the VisaCard

- American engineer Jack Kilby of Texas Instruments designs the first true integrated circuit

1959

- The first U.S. nuclear-powered merchant vessel, *Savannah*, goes into service

- Mattel, Inc., makes the first Barbie doll

- Haloid Xerox introduces plain paper copier

- Holiday gift purchases include the KitchenAid portable dishwasher, Hoover Electric Floor Washer, General Electric automatic can opener and Westinghouse Dog-O-Matic hot dog cooker

- Sperry Rand and RCA co-produce the first fully transistorized computer

Mylar strands hold a 3-ton car, 1955

Syntex scientists examine a pile of barbasco root from which cortisone is synthesized

1960

- Mobil Oil forms Mobil Chemical Co., which is among the 15 largest chemical operations in the U.S.

- Westvaco introduces its Printkote bleached paperboard, the first low density bleached paperboard; this innovation greatly increased efficiency and graphic quality in the production of consumer product packaging

- Construction of McCormick Place Exposition Center in Chicago, site of the annual National Manufacturing Week exposition, which is sponsored by the NAM and Reed Exhibition Company

- The first meteorological satellite, *Tiros I*, is launched by U.S. and sends back pictures of the Earth's cloud cover

- Transistors are used to replace valves in commercial computers by the Digital Equipment Corporation; Sony develops first all-transistor portable TV

- Bison Gear and Engineering Corp., of Downers Grove, Illinois, is founded

- Digital Equipment Corporation introduces the world's first small, interactive computer, PDP-1

- AT&T applies for a permit to launch the first communications satellite and tests its first electronic switching service, which would be phased in during the years to come

- Ingersoll-Rand introduces the Crawlmaster

- Sony establishes its first major overseas operation in New York City. Known today as Sony Electronics Inc., it celebrates $1 million in sales in its first year

- Newport News Shipbuilding launches the first nuclear-powered aircraft carrier, the USS *Enterprise*

1961

- The first manned U.S. space flight is made by Alan Shepard

- Time-sharing computer introduced at MIT

- Ray Kroc borrows $2.7 million to buy out McDonald brothers

- NU-MIRROR of Depew, New York, a division of Yeager Industries, Inc., begins mass producing low cost parts for auto glass manufacturers

- The first electric toothbrush is launched

- The incredibly strong steel alloy, Maraging, is introduced

- President Kennedy's address to the NAM helps build support for the Trade Expansion Act of 1962

Mercury astronaut Scott Carpenter's launch televised in New York City's Grand Central Station

1962

- U.S. astronauts Glenn, Carpenter and Schirra all orbit the earth separately

- First communications satellite, Telstar, is launched from Cape Canaveral, establishing transatlantic television programs

- *Mariner 2* launched by U.S. as Venus probe

- U.S. has 200 atomic reactors in operation

- IBM introduces disk storage systems for computers

1963

- Powered into space by the Atlas rocket, U.S. astronaut Gordon Cooper and his capsule complete 22 orbits of the earth

- The first artificial heart is used to take over the circulation of a patient's blood during heart surgery

- Eveready invents lithium technology

- Hyde Park Electronics, Inc., of Dayton, Ohio, is founded

1964

- Sara Lee opens the first fully-automated factory which uses computer-operated equipment

- The omega-minus elementary particle, predicted by theory, is discovered at Brookhaven National Laboratory, Upton, New York, launching the search for more elusive subatomic particles

- *Ranger VII* yields close-up photographs of the moon's surface

- Verrazano-Narrows Bridge, the world's longest single-span suspension bridge, opens to traffic in New York

Mercury-Atlas 6 rocket carrying John Glenn

1965

- AT&T 800 service introduced
- The silicon chip is introduced in the U.S.
- U.S. astronaut Edward White walks from Gemini 4 for 21 minutes
- Kevlar, a tough, lightweight synthetic fiber that resists stretching, is discovered by Stephanie Kwolek at DuPont; five times stronger than steel and three times stiffer than fiberglass, Kevlar fiber is now used for bullet-proof vests
- Bethlehem Steel develops a method of pre-fabricating parallel-wire strands for suspension bridge cables

Chevrolet assembly line, 1965

1966

- The first system to make solderless, simultaneous connection of multiple wires, called CHAMP, is released by AMP Inc. in labor-saving connectors for 25-pair cable used by the telephone industry
- U.S. spacecraft *Surveyor 1* makes soft landings on the moon
- U.S. astronaut Edwin E. Aldrin, Jr., steps out of the Gemini 12 spacecraft for 129 minutes

1967

- Tenneco Inc. expands and diversifies by acquiring major interests in agriculture and land management, automotive parts and agricultural and construction equipment
- Texas Instruments Inc. invents hand-held calculator
- Amana introduces countertop microwave oven
- The U.S. nuclear-powered submarine fleet now consists of 74 boats
- After the deaths of three astronauts in a fire on a launching pad, U.S. manned space lights are temporarily suspended
- The U.S. has 100 million telephones in service
- Stone Construction Equipment of Honeoye, New York, a leader in the design, manufacture and marketing of light construction equipment, is founded
- A synthetic version of DNA is produced by biochemists at Stanford University

1968

- Violence and rioting escalate in numerous cities, reinforcing a gradual, long-term trend toward suburbanization and some manufacturing facilities locating outside of inner cities
- U.S. spacecraft *Surveyor 7* lands successfully on the moon
- Apollo 8 spacecraft is launched from Cape Kennedy, Florida, and orbits the moon
- Intelsat 3A, the first of a new series of communication satellites, is launched
- Cable television is introduced
- Nucor Corporation in Charlotte, North Carolina, begins operations
- Intel Corporation is established
- LTV Corporation purchases Jones & Laughlin Steel

1969

- On July 20, Neil Armstrong and Edwin "Buzz" Aldrin become the first men to walk on the moon as Michael Collins, the third astronaut aboard the historic Apollo 11 flight, orbits above them
- The U.S. government removes cyclamates from the market and limits the use of monosodium glutamate
- Pictures of the surface of Mars are sent back to earth by two *Mariner* space probes
- Approximately 225 million telephones are in service all over the world, 114 million in the U.S.
- Landa Systems of Portland, Oregon, is founded
- MasterCard is introduced
- The Concorde, Anglo-French supersonic aircraft, makes its first test flight
- Storage Technology Corporation begins operations

AT&T introduces its Touch-Tone phone, 1963

1970

- The Boeing 747 jumbo jet begins passenger service

- Verbatim Corporation, incorporated as Information Terminals Corp., begins marketing the first data cassette built to ANSI standards

- The first complete synthesis of a gene occurs at the University of Wisconsin

- The 150-inch reflecting telescope at Kitt Peak Observatory, Tucson, Arizona, is completed

- The world production of crude steel reaches 595 million metric tons

- Electronic Controls Co. (ECCO), a manufacturer of back-up alarms, is founded

1971

- Microprocessor (logic and arithmetic unit of a computer on a single silicon chip) patented by the Intel Corporation; first pocket calculators become commercially available in the U.S.

- McDonnell Douglas' first DC-10 jets go into use

- Quadraphonic sound, with four separate sound signals, is introduced

- U.S. satellite, *Mariner 9*, orbits Mars

- American astronomers discover two "new" galaxies adjacent to the earth's own galaxy, the Milky Way

- Amtrak begins to operate U.S. passenger railroads

- Bausch & Lomb introduces soft contact lenses

- The American Society of Mechanical Engineers forms a committee to initiate a historical program to recognize historically significant mechanical engineering artifacts

- Meteorologists use Doppler radar to watch storm systems

1972

- Hewlett-Packard produces HP-35, the world's first hand-held scientific calculator

- Apollo 16 astronauts spend 71 hours on the surface of the moon

- *Life* magazine ceases publication

- The CAT-scan is introduced

- AMP Inc. provides connectors with Action Pin Contacts that need no soldering for reliable connection to printed circuit boards, for simpler manufacturing processes

- Intel introduces the 4004 microprocessor

1973

- The energy crisis is in full swing

- The water cannon is first used in the construction industry to fracture rock by spraying water at pressures of up to 650,000 lbs/square inch

- Universal Product Code is introduced, enabling retail scanning and source identification by laser

- Xerox unveils its 3100 compact copier, capable of making 20 copies per minute

- The National Screw Machine Products Association of Brecksville, Ohio, celebrates its centennial

- The American Skylab I, II and III space missions are completed successfully

- TV pictures are transmitted by American space probe *Pioneer 10* within 81,000 miles of the planet Jupiter

- Sharp introduces calculators with LCDs

1974

- Parker Hannifin Corporation of Cleveland, Ohio, becomes the first manufacturer to use Kevlar for reinforcing hydraulic hose

- The NAM moves its headquarters from New York City to Washington, D.C., to enhance its lobbying and government relations operations

- U.S. Skylab III astronauts spend 84 days in space

- U.S. *Mariner 10* satellite transmits detailed pictures of both Venus and Mercury

- Lockheed's SR-71 Blackbird jet plane flies from New York to London in one hour 55 minutes and 42 seconds and reaches speeds of 2,000 mph

AMP Inc.'s Action Pin Contacts which need no soldering for reliable press-fit connections to printed circuit boards, 1972

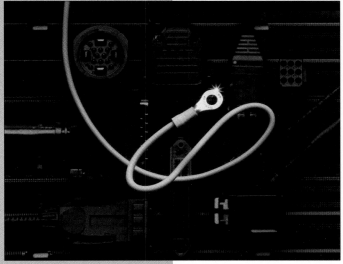

AMP Incorporated's solderless connector today

1975

- 3M begins its 3P (Pollution Prevention Pays) program, spawning more then 4,100 projects that reduced corporate pollution

- Personal and affordable computers begin to appear, launching another computer revolution that brings the machines into homes and schools, as well as into every aspect of business

- Unemployment rate in the U.S. reaches 9.2 percent, highest since 1941

- Miller Electric Manufacturing Company markets the Syncrowave power source, used by many for aluminum and stainless steel welding

- Environmentally friendly non-detachable beverage can openers appear; in broad use by 1979

- The cost of mailing a first-class letter in the U.S. increases from 10 cents to 13 cents

- Sony establishes a Trinitron television manufacturing facility in San Diego, California, and becomes the first Japanese electronics company to manufacture televisions in the U.S.

Electronic Controls Co.'s Smart Alarm, 1980

1976

- Americans celebrate the nation's bicentennial

- Landing vehicles from U.S. spacecrafts *Viking I* and *II* set down safely on Mars and transmit the first close-up photos of its surface

- Cray Research builds first supercomputer: Cray-1

- The Lockheed SR-71 Blackbird plane sets seven new world speed and altitude records, breaking several records previously held by Soviet Union planes

1977

- Seventy thousand workers complete the 799-mile Trans-Alaskan pipeline, built at a cost of $9 billion, facilitating the environmentally sound flow of vital energy from Prudhoe Bay

- Tenneco Inc. further expands its operations by acquiring an automotive ride-control business and 40 percent of a France-based construction equipment firm

- U.S. unmanned spacecrafts *Voyager I* and *II* begin journeys to explore outer solar system

- The structure of the sun's magnetic field is determined for the first time from data returned by the U.S. *Pioneer II* spacecraft

- Passenger service on the Concorde supersonic transport begins between New York, Paris and London

- Oracle Systems Corporation is founded

1978

- Raymond Damadian founds FONAR Corporation to manufacture the MRI scanner, which would receive FDA approval in 1984

- Intel invents the 8088 microcomputer chip

- NAM lobbying helps secure the decisive defeat of a sweeping and ill-advised labor law "reform" bill

- World's population stands at about 4.4 billion persons, with 200,000 being added daily

- Genentech clones first recombinant DNA product, human insulin

- The first "test-tube baby" is born in England

1979

- A ring around Jupiter is discovered by the *Voyager I* spacecraft

- The personal stereo or "Walkman" is introduced by Sony

- The NAM becomes the first major business group to press for a national industrial revitalization effort; the Association distributes 437,000 brochures describing the NAM's plan, major elements of which were enacted in 1981

- Grumman Corporation marks its 50th anniversary — now Northrop Grumman

The Trans-Alaskan pipeline carries oil from Prudhoe Bay to Valdez, supplying energy for the lower 48 states

1980

- The nation endures a weak economy and the Iran Hostage Crisis

- Eveready's Energizer is introduced

- *Voyager I* space probe sends back spectacular photographs of Saturn, its moons and rings; six new moons are discovered

- The eradication of smallpox is announced by the World Health Organization

- A ruling that a microbe created by General Electric to eliminate oil waste can be patented is upheld by the U.S. Supreme Court

- I.C.I. begins production of the world's first commercially available animal foodstuff to be made from micro-organisms

- Armstrong World Industries, with roots dating to 1860, adopts its current name

Art Fry of 3M

1981

- IBM launches its "home" or "personal" computer (PC)

- NASA launches and lands Rockwell International Corporation's Space Shuttle *Columbia*

- FDA approves the first transdermal product, Ciba-Geigy's Transderm Scop, developed by Alza Corporation, which continuously treats motion sickness

- Scientists identify Acquired Immune Deficiency Syndrome (AIDS); first unrecognized cases date from late 1970s

- Surgeons at University of Denver insert a valve into the skull of an unborn baby to drain excess fluid from the brain and prevent hydrocephalus

- Birth of Elizabeth Carr, first test-tube baby in U.S.

1982

- A recession leads to higher unemployment and difficult times in many regions and industries

- Notwithstanding a deep recession, The Timken Company breaks ground on the first new alloy steel plant to be built in the United States in a generation; the plant, which drew a visit from President Reagan, opened in 1985 and became the first steel plant ever cited as one of America's best plants by *Industry Week*

- The first commercial product of genetic engineering appears when human insulin produced by bacteria is marketed

- The first private space rocket (the *Conestoga 1*) makes a sub-orbital flight

- Combined heart-lung and kidney-pancreas transplants are carried out successfully

- The first Jarvik 7 artificial heart is successfully implanted

- Newport News Shipbuilding becomes the first shipyard to deliver two major U.S. Navy vessels in a single day — the aircraft carrier *Carl Vinson* and the attack submarine *Atlanta*

- Sun Microsystems, Inc., is founded

1983

- MCI orders first big fiber-optic system from Corning and Siecor

- Ameritech receives FCC's first cellular phone license

- Amgen's Dr. Fu Kuen Lin isolates and clones the gene for human erythropoietin. This discovery prompted construction of the EPOGEN manufacturing facility

- PPG Industries of Pittsburgh, Pennsylvania, celebrates its centennial

- Cooper Industries of Houston, Texas, marks its 150th anniversary

- OTC drug packaging practices change in response to 1982 cyanide tampering with bottled Tylenol

- U.S. Space Shuttle *Challenger* is launched

- The U.S. government approves the use of aspartame as an artificial sweetener in soft drinks

- Gene markers that identify Duchenne muscular dystrophy and Huntington's Disease are identified

- The compact disc is launched, leading to enhanced music quality

- Cyclosporine is licensed, a drug that reduces the body's tendency to reject foreign tissue; heart transplants proliferated

- President Reagan signs Social Security reform plan recommended by commission whose membership includes NAM President Alexander B. Trowbridge

1984

- Peavey Electronics Corporation manufactures its first digital powered amplifier: DECA 700

- Chevron begins its SMART (Save Money and Reduce Toxics) plan

- Westvaco becomes the first company to commercialize dual ovenable packaging which allows frozen foods to be packaged, shipped, displayed and heated in a microwave or conventional oven in a single carton

- The Apple Macintosh microcomputer with mouse is launched

- A silicon microchip is developed that can store four times more data than previously possible

- The first astronauts to walk in space untethered using backpacks are Bruce McCandless and Robert Stewart

- The space shuttle *Discovery* successfully makes its maiden flight

- A world record of 71,830 patents are filed in the U.S.

- U.S. funds research for new space-based defense system, the Strategic Defense Initiative, envisioned using lasers and particle-beam weapons to destroy incoming hostile missiles

- The Institute of Electrical and Electronics Engineers (IEEE) celebrates its centennial

1985

- Intel 386 chip becomes available
- Microsoft Windows debuts, making computer use easier for many
- Marion Merrell Dow Inc. has Seldane approved, the first non-sedating antihistamine for the treatment of seasonal allergies
- General Motors sets up Saturn, a far-reaching experiment in carmaking
- Researchers develop new technique for sending up to 300,000 phone calls through one fiber optic cable at the same time
- M. A. Hanna Co., of Cleveland, Ohio, marks its centennial
- Surgeons use lasers to clean out clogged arteries
- Amstrad launches the PCW 8256 word processor
- Johnson Controls, Inc., marks its centennial
- Hussey Seating marks its 150th anniversary

1986

- Dow Chemical launches its WRAP (Waste Reduction Always Pays) program
- U.S. scientists discover the first gene known to inhibit growth (in this case it inhibits the cancer retinoblastoma)
- The lightweight airplane *Voyager* makes the first nonstop flight around the world without refueling, taking nine days
- Hoffman-LaRoche launches its first genetically engineered product, Roferon A
- Trinova Corporation, manufacturers and distributors of engineered components and systems for industry, is founded
- The Coca-Cola Company celebrates its centennial
- Dart & Kraft sells some of its subsidiaries, leading to the establishment of Premark International, Inc.

1987

- The 25th anniversary of the launch of the Telestar communications satellite; 3.6 billion telephone calls have now been relayed by communications satellites
- Bill Gates, founder of Microsoft, becomes microcomputing's first billionaire
- America's Cup winner *Stars and Stripes* uses sails made of Kevlar
- New Jersey adopts first statewide recycling law
- National Can Company and American Can Company merge to form American National Can Company
- Computer technology meets public policy as the NAM launches NAMnet: The Public Policy Electronic Network

1988

- Facsimile machine takes off in U.S., selling more than 1 million units; the original concept patented by Scotsman Alexander Bain in 1845, but it took miniaturization of components to popularize the device
- Hewlett-Packard develops the DeskJet printer
- Tenneco Inc. sells its Tenneco Oil Company division and uses the proceeds of about $7 billion to retire debt and repurchase shares of common stock
- A new Rocco, Inc. chicken hatchery opens with 700,000 chicks hatched per week — or 36 million chicks hatched in a year
- The FDA approves Upjohn's Rogaine for treating baldness; the compound was first developed as an antacid in 1958 but received FDA approval as an anti-hypertensive in 1979
- The first transatlantic optical fiber telephone cable links France, the U.K. and the U.S.
- The American Boiler Manufacturers Association, celebrates its centennial
- Chisholm, Boyd & White Company of Alsip, Illinois, celebrates its centennial

1989

- Intel 486 chip hits the market
- Computer viruses infect worldwide computer networks
- A declaration is adopted by 80 nations agreeing to stop producing chlorofluorocarbons (CFCs), which damage the world's ozone layer
- Lotus Notes groupware offered
- Carpenter Technology Corp. of Reading, Pennsylvania, celebrates its centennial

Giddings & Lewis lathes old and new

F-117 Stealth Fighter

1990

- The first low-calorie fat substitute is approved by the Food and Drug Administration
- A young girl becomes the first human to receive gene therapy
- The Hubble space telescope goes into orbit
- Emerson Electric Co., maker of electric motors and other fine electric products, marks its centennial

1991

- A Tufts University study shows pharmaceutical manufacturers are the source of 92 percent of new drugs, with government and academia accounting for 8 percent
- Raytheon's Patriot missile defense system works successfully during the Persian Gulf War
- Compact disks outsell cassettes
- Tenneco Inc. begins major transformation by instituting an action plan to sell non-core assets, reduce quarterly dividends, issue new equity, reduce capital spending and lower operating costs
- Peavey Electronics Corporation is selected as one of 20 U.S. companies to participate in the "Japan Corporate Program," sponsored by the U.S. Department of Commerce

The Timken Company's Faircrest Steel Plant, which marked its 10th anniversary in 1995

1992

- Worzalla Publishing Company celebrates its centennial
- Square D supplies electrical distribution and control products for the Baltimore Orioles' baseball park at Camden Yards
- The Stanley Works celebrates its 150th anniversary and Medusa Corp. marks its centennial

1993

- Intel Pentium chip is introduced
- General Electric introduces Genesis Series 1 passenger locomotives for Amtrak
- Tenneco's Newport News Shipbuilding launches the *John C. Stennis* (CVN-74) nuclear-powered aircraft carrier
- Alza's Testoderm system is cleared for marketing
- NASA selects Boeing Defense and Space Group as the prime contractor for the space station

1994

- ADM, Asphalt Drum Mixers, Inc., of Huntertown, Indiana, sells the first American drum mix plant to Russia
- The Timken Company produces its 10-millionth all-purpose railroad bearing
- Case Corporation goes public
- Tenneco Inc. makes substantial domestic and international investments in natural gas transportation and marketing, packaging and automotive parts
- The Boeing Company unveils 777: the largest twin-jet airplane ever built
- Eaton Corp. acquires Westinghouse's electric controls business
- Newport News Shipbuilding becomes the first American shipyard to obtain a commercial construction contract from an international shipowner since 1957
- Sony Electronics Inc.'s San Diego Manufacturing Center is selected as one of America's ten best plants by *Industry Week* magazine and becomes the first television and computer display manufacturing operation to ever receive this recognition

1995

- The NAM celebrates its centennial
- FCC begins auctioning broadband spectrum licenses for personal communications services
- Northrop Grumman Corporation, the principal subcontractor on the Navy's first F/A-18 Hornet, completes and delivers its section of the Hornet strike fighter to McDonnell Douglas
- Brooklyn Union Gas Co. celebrates its centennial
- Gibson Greetings celebrates its centennial
- Glenshaw Glass Co. marks its centennial
- Harris Corporation celebrates its centennial
- Lennox International Inc. celebrates its centennial
- Westvaco introduces a new version of its NUCHAR activated carbon, enabling automobile manufacturers to meet stringent 1995 pollution control requirements
- Stow Manufacturing Company of Binghamton, New York, celebrates its 120th anniversary
- The Lincoln Electric Company, celebrating its own centennial, opens its new motor division facility, which manufactures high-quality electric motors
- Sony Electronics Inc. commences production of computer display cathode ray tubes at its plant in San Diego, California, and becomes the only U.S. manufacturer of color picture tubes for computer displays
- More than 65,000 people visit the National Manufacturing Week expo, sponsored by the NAM and Reed Exhibition Co. in Chicago

Newport News Shipbuilding & Dry Dock Co. launching the *John C. Stennis*, 1993

Since its founding in 1895, The National Association of Manufacturers has had close ties with the many state and local manufacturing and industry associations, industry-specific associations and employer associations. These fine associations are members of the National Industrial Council and the Associations Council. The NAM is proud of its long-standing relationship with these associations.

National Industrial Council — Employer Association Group

Community Relations Association, Inc.
Arizona Employers' Council, Inc.
California Association of Employers
The Employers Group
  Los Angeles, CA
Sacramento Valley Employers' Council
  Sacramento, CA
San Diego Employers Association, Inc.
  San Diego, CA
Mountain States Employers Council,
  Inc., Denver, CO
AAIM, The Management Association
  North Haven, CT
Norwalk Manufacturers Council
  Norwalk, CT
Manufacturing Alliance of Connecticut,
  Inc., Stratford, CT
The Western Connecticut Industrial
  Council, Inc., Waterbury, CT
Employers Association of Florida
South Florida Manufacturers
  Association, Pompano Beach, FL
Florida Employers' Council, Inc.
  Venice, FL
Georgia Employers' Association
Pacific Management Resources Group
  Agana, Guam
Hawaii Employers Council
IEC Management Resource Group
  Boise, ID
Associated Employers, Moline, IL
Employers' Association of Illinois
  Peoria, IL
The Management Association of Illinois
  Broadview, IL
Northern Illinois Business Association
  Buffalo Grove, IL
Southwestern Illinois Industrial
  Association, Wood River, IL
Valley Industrial Association, Aurora, IL
The Employers Association, Inc.
  Braintree, MA
CMEA The Employers Association
  Worcester, MA
Employers Association of Western
  Massachusetts, Inc., Ludlow, MA

The Employers' Association
  Grand Rapids, MI
American Society of Employers
  Southfield, MI
Employers Association of West
  Michigan, Muskegon, MI
Employers Association, Inc.
  Minneapolis, MN
Northeast Mississippi Community
  Relations Association
Associated Employers of Montana
Nevada Association of Employers
AAIM Management Association
  St. Louis, MO
Employers Association of New Jersey
  Verona, NJ
IMA-Management Association, Inc.
  Clifton, NJ
Council of Industry of Southeastern
  New York, New Paltz, NY
Industrial Management Council
  Rochester, NY
MACNY The Employer Association
  Syracuse, NY
Capital Associated Industries, Inc.
  Raleigh, NC
Piedmont Associated Industries
  Greensboro, NC
The Employers Association
  Charlotte, NC
Western Carolina Industries, Inc.
  Asheville, NC
Employers Resource Association, Inc.
  Cincinnati, OH
Employers Resource Council
  Seven Hills, OH
Associated Employers of Central Ohio
  Columbus, OH
The Employers' Association
  Sylvania, OH
The Manufacturers Association of
  Eastern Ohio and Western
  Pennsylvania, Warren, OH
Cascade Employers Association, Inc.
  of the Pacific Northwest, Salem, OR
Timber Operators Council, Inc.
  Tigard, OR
United Employers Association
  Portland, OR

Manufacturers Association of Berks
  County, Reading, PA
MidAtlantic Employers Association
  Valley Forge, PA
Manufacturers Association of Mid-
  Eastern Pennsylvania, Pottsville, PA
Manufacturers' Association of
  Northeastern Pennsylvania
  West Pittston, PA
Manufacturers Association of
  Northwest Pennsylvania, Erie, PA
Manufacturers Association of South
  Central Pennsylvania, York, PA
TEC/Pennsylvania Small Business
  United, Pittsburgh, PA
West Branch Manufacturers'
  Association, Montoursville, PA
Spartanburg Development Association
  Spartanburg, SC
IRC-The Employers Council
  Salt Lake City, UT
Central Virginia Industries, Inc.
  Lynchburg, VA
The Management Association of
  Western Virginia, Roanoke, VA
Associated Industries, Spokane, WA
Timber Products Manufacturers
  Spokane, WA
Washington Employers, Inc.
  Seattle, WA
Kenosha Manufacturers and Employers
  Association, Kenosha, WI
MRA-The Management Association,
  Inc., Brookfield, WI
Racine Area Manufacturers and
  Commerce (RAMAC), Racine, WI

National Industrial Council — State Associations Group

Business Council of Alabama
Arizona Association of Industries
Associated Industries of Arkansas, Inc.
California Manufacturers Association
Colorado Association of Commerce &
  Industry
Connecticut Business & Industry
  Association, Inc.
Delaware State Chamber of Commerce
Associated Industries of Florida
Georgia Chamber of Commerce
Manufacturers Association of Hawaii

Idaho Association of Commerce &
  Industry
Illinois Manufacturers' Association
Indiana Manufacturers Association, Inc.
Iowa Association of Business &
  Industry
Kansas Chamber of Commerce &
  Industry
Associated Industries of Kentucky
Louisiana Association of Business &
  Industry
Maine Chamber of Commerce &
  Industry
Maryland Chamber of Commerce
Associated Industries of
  Massachusetts
Michigan Manufacturers Association
Minnesota Chamber of Commerce &
  Industry
Mississippi Manufacturers Association
Associated Industries of Missouri
Nebraska Chamber of Commerce &
  Industry
Nevada Manufacturers Association
Business and Industry Association of
  New Hampshire
New Jersey Business and Industry
  Association
Association of Commerce and Industry
  of New Mexico
Business Council of New York State,
  Inc.
Greater North Dakota Association
Ohio Manufacturers' Association
Oklahoma State Chamber of
  Commerce and Industry
Associated Oregon Industries, Inc.
Pennsylvania Manufacturers'
  Association
Puerto Rico Manufacturers Association
South Carolina Chamber of Commerce
Industry & Commerce Association of
  South Dakota
Tennessee Association of Business
Texas Association of Business and
  Chambers of Commerce
Utah Manufacturers Association
Associated Industries of Vermont
Virginia Manufacturers Association
Association of Washington Business
West Virginia Manufacturers
  Association
Wisconsin Manufacturers & Commerce

Associations Council of the National Association of Manufacturers

The Adhesive and Sealant Council
Aerospace Industries Association of
  America
AIM USA
Air-Conditioning and Refrigeration
  Institute
The Aluminum Association
Aluminum Extruders Council
American Automobile Manufacturers
  Association
American Bearing Manufacturers
  Association
American Boiler Manufacturers
  Association
American Coke and Coal Chemicals
  Institute
American Dental Trade Association
American Electronics Association
American Feed Industry Association
American Fiber Manufacturers
  Association
American Forest & Paper Association
American Foundrymen's Society
American Furniture Manufacturers
  Association
American Gas Association
American Gear Manufacturers
  Association
American Hardware Manufacturers
  Association
American Health and Beauty Aids
  Institute
American Institute of Steel
  Construction
American Iron & Steel Institute
American Lighting Association
American Meat Institute
American Petroleum Institute
American Pipe Fittings Association
American Plastics Council
American Portland Cement Alliance
American Pulpwood Association

American Shooting Sports Council

American Supply & Machinery Manufacturers Association

American Textile Machinery Association

American Textile Manufacturers Institute

American Waterways Shipyard Conference

American Wire Producers Association

American Wood Preservers Institute

American Zinc Association

AMT-The Association for Manufacturing Technology

Arkansas Wood Manufacturers Association

Asphalt Institute

Asphalt Roofing Manufacturers Association

Association of Home Appliance Manufacturers

Association of Independent Corrugated Converters

Association of International Automobile Manufacturers

Battery Council International

BEMA, An International Association Serving the Baking and Food Industries

Biscuit and Cracker Manufacturers' Association

Book Manufacturers Institute

Brick Institute of America

Builders Hardware Manufacturers Association

Business & Institutional Furniture Manufacturers Association

Business Products Industry Association

Can Manufacturers Institute

Carpet and Rug Institute

Ceramic Manufacturers Association

Certified Ballast Manufacturers

Chemical Manufacturers Association

Chemical Specialties Manufacturers Association

The Chlorine Institute

Color Pigments Manufacturers Association

Commercial Refrigerator Manufacturers Association

Composite Can and Tube Institute

Compressed Gas Association

Computer and Communications Industry Association

Construction Industry Manufacturers Association

Conveyor Equipment Manufacturers Association

Copper and Brass Fabricators Council

Cosmetic, Toiletry and Fragrance Association

Council on Superconductivity

Distilled Spirits Council of the U.S.

Edison Electric Institute

Electricity Consumers Resource Council

Electronic Design Automation Companies

Electronic Industries Association

Electronic Messaging Association

Envelope Manufacturers Association of America

Environmental Industry Associations

Equipment Manufacturers Institute

Fibre Box Association

Fire and Emergency Manufacturers and Services Association

Fire Apparatus Manufacturers Association

Flexible Packaging Association

Food Processing Machinery & Supplies Association

Foodservice and Packaging Institute

Footwear Industries of America

Forging Industry Association

Gas Appliance Manufacturers Association

Generic Pharmaceutical Industry Association

Glass Packaging Institute

Grocery Manufacturers of America

Gypsum Association

Hardwood Manufacturers Association

Hardwood Plywood and Veneer Association

Health Industry Manufacturers Association

Hearing Industries Association

Hearth Products Association

Hobby Industry Association

Hydraulic Institute

IBFI, The International Association Serving the Forms, Information Management, Systems Automation and Printed Communications Requirements of Business

Industrial Heating Equipment Association

Industrial Safety Equipment Association

Industrial Truck Association

Information Technology Association of America

Information Technology Industry Council

Institute for Interconnecting and Packaging Electronic Circuits

Institute of Clean Air Companies

Institute of Makers of Explosives

International Bottled Water Association

International Cadmium Association

International Dairy Foods Association

International Sanitary Supply Association

International Sign Association

Kitchen Cabinet Manufacturers Association

Lead Industries Association

Leather Industries of America

The Lignin Institute

Machine Knife Association

Manufactured Housing Institute

Manufacturing Jewelers and Silversmiths of America

Metal Building Manufacturers Association

Metal Treating Institute

Michigan Tooling Association

Motor and Equipment Manufacturers Association

National Association of Band Instrument Manufacturers

National Association of Garage Door Manufacturers

National Association of Hosiery Manufacturers

National Association of Mirror Manufacturers

National Association of Music Merchants

National Association of Photographic Manufacturers

National Association of Relay Manufacturers

National Association of Store Fixture Manufacturers

National Clay Pipe Institute

National Coil Coaters Association

National Corrugated Steel Pipe Association

National Electrical Manufacturers Association

National Fluid Power Association

National Glass Association

National Housewares Manufacturers Association

National Independent Energy Producers

National Industrial Sand Association

National Industries for the Blind

National Lime Association

National Marine Manufacturers Association

National Mining Association

National Ocean Industries Association

National Oilseed Processors Association

National Paperbox Association

National Precast Concrete Association

National Propane Gas Association

National Screw Machine Products Association

National Soft Drink Association

Natural Gas Supply Association

Non-Ferrous Founders' Society

Nonprescription Drug Manufacturers Association

North American Association of Food Equipment Manufacturers

North American Insulation Manufacturers Association

NPES, The Association for Suppliers of Printing and Publishing Technologies

Nuclear Energy Institute

Optical Industry Association

Outdoor Power Equipment Institute

Packaging Machinery Manufacturers Institute

Paperboard Packaging Council

Pet Food Institute

Pharmaceutical Research and Manufacturers of America

Plumbing Manufacturers Institute

Polyisocyanurate Insulation Manufacturers Association

Portable Power Equipment Manufacturers Association

Portland Cement Association

Power Sources Manufacturers Association

Power Tool Institute

Power Transmission Distributors Association

Precision Metalforming Association

Pressure Sensitive Tape Council

Private Label Manufacturers Association

Process Equipment Manufacturers' Association

The Refractories Institute

Roof Coatings Manufacturers Association

Rubber Manufacturers Association

SAMA Group of Associations/Analytical Instrument Association

Secondary Materials and Recycled Textiles

Security Industry Association

Semiconductor Industry Association

Shipbuilders Council of America

SMMA, The Association for Electric Motors, Their Control and Application

Society of Glass and Ceramic Decorators

Society of the Plastics Industry

Sporting Goods Manufacturers Association

Spring Manufacturers Institute

Steel Manufacturers Association

Steel Plate Fabricators Association

Steel Service Center Institute

Steel Shipping Container Institute

Steel Tank Institute

Synthetic Organic Chemical Manufacturers Association

Telecommunications Industry Association

Textile Care Allied Trades Association

Tobacco Institute

Toy Manufacturers of America

U.S. Cutting Tool Institute

U.S. Industrial Fabrics Institute

Valve Manufacturers Association of America

Water and Wastewater Equipment Manufacturers Association

Waterbed Council

Western & English Manufacturers Association

Wirebound Box Manufacturers Association

Wiring Harness Manufacturers Association

Wood Machinery Manufacturers of America

Writing Instrument Manufacturers Association

Index

A

Abbott Laboratories, 137
Acme-Cleveland Corporation, 136
Adams, J. D., 136
Aiken, Howard, 85
Air-Conditioning and Refrigeration Institute, 147
Air Conditioning, 35
Air Products and Chemicals Inc., 146
Alabama Laser Technologies, **111**
Alcan Aluminum Corporation, 147
Aldrin, Edwin E. "Buzz", 107, **107**
Alexanderson, Ernst, 139
Allegheny International Corporation, 136
Allis Chalmers, 55, 81
Aluminum, 31
Aluminum Association, 143
Aluminum Company of America (Alcoa), 31, **31**, 138, 139
Alza Corporation, 153, 155
Amana Refrigeration, Inc., 114, 150
American Association of Pharmaceutical Chemists, 138
American Boiler Manufacturers Association, 154
American Cyanamid Company, 138
American Express Company, 95, **95**
American Farm Bureau, 140
American Federation of Labor, 59
American Greetings Corporation, 138
American Institute of Chemical Engineers, 138
American Institute of Steel Construction, 141
American National Can Company, 154
American Racine Universal Motor Company, 141
American Society of Mechanical Engineers, 151
American Textile Machinery Association, 143
Ameritech, 153
Amgen, Inc., **3**, **117**, 153
AMP, Inc., 146, 148, 150, 151, **151**
Amstrad, 154
Amtrak, 151
Anderson, Walter, 115
A&P (Great Atlantic and Pacific Tea Co.), 43
Apple Computer, Inc., 112, 126, 153
Archbold Industries, 136
Armstrong, Neil A., 104, 107
Armstrong World Industries, 153
Artificial Intelligence (AI), 121
Asphalt Drum Mixers, Inc. (ADM), 155
Assembly line, 26, 28, 96
Atlas missile, 101
AT&T, 46, 101, 106, 138, 142, 147, 148, 149, 150, **150**; Western Electric, 97, 138, 142; *See also* Bell Labs
Atomic bomb. *See* Manhattan Project
Atomic energy, 100, **100**
Atomic Energy Commission, 100, 146, 147
Aureomycin, 94, 146
Automatic Hook and Eye Company, 140

Automatic Machinery and Tool Company, 138
Automobile, 28, 29, **29**, 42, 44, 89; industry, 29, 44, 72
Aviation, 27, 30, 31, 42, 101; air travel, 50, 62, 89, 108; helicopter, 65; aircraft industry, 76, 89, 101, 108

B

Babbage, Charles, 85
Babson, Roger, 43
Baekeland, Leo, 32, **32**, 138
Bakelite, 32, **32**, 137
Ball, F. C., 136
Bank of America, 95, 148
Bardeen, John, 97
Bauer, Inc., Eddie, 141
Bausch & Lomb, 142, 151
Becket, F. M., 137
Beech Nut, 143
Bell, Alexander Graham, 46, 140
Bell Aircraft Corporation, 101, **101**, 146
Bell & Howell Company, 49, **49**, 92
Bell Labs, 97, 110, 138, 142, 144, 146, 147; *See also* AT&T
Bessemer process, 16
Best Tractor Co., C. L. *See* Caterpillar, Inc.
Bethlehem Steel Company, **25**, 32, **39**, 79, 145, 150
Birds Eye brand. *See* General Foods Corporation
Birdseye, Clarence, 66, **66**, 141
Bison Gear and Engineering Corp., 149
Black & Decker Corporation, 36
Bob's Candies, Inc., 147
Boeing Company, The, 30, 50, 72, 140, 155; B & W Model 1, 30, 140, **30**; B-17 Flying Fortress, *72*; B-29 Super fortress, *72*, 76, **76**, 101; Boeing *747*, 108, **108**, 151; Boeing *777*, 155
Boeing, William E., 30, 140
Brattain, Walter, 97
Briggs & Stratton Corporation, 138
Brooklyn Union Gas Co., 155
Brunswick Corporation, 92, **92**, 148
Budd Manufacturing Company, Edward G., 63
Buick Motor Division, General Motors Corporation, **29**, 142
Burger King, 147
Burton, W. M., 139
Bush, Vannevar, 85
Butler Manufacturing Company, 144
Byers Co., A. M., 143

C

CAD (computer-aided design), 119, 122, **122**
Cadillac Motor Division, 139
CAM (computer-aided manufacturing), 119, 122
CAT scan (computerized axial tomography), 105, 124, **124**, 144

Campbell Soup Company, **11**, 23, **23**, 136, 139
Capek, Karel, 121
Carlson, Chester F., 96, 144
Carothers, Wallace H., 60, 144
Carpenter Technology Corp., 154
Carrier, Willis Haviland, 35
Carrier Corporation, 35
Carver, George Washington, 136
Case Corporation, **54**, 55, **55**, 78, **78**, 139, 141, 148, 155; Case Motor Works, 139
Caterpillar Inc., **54**, 55, 137
Cellophane. *See* DuPont
Cellular telephone, 123
Chase Manhattan Bank, 136
Chevrolet Motor Division, General Motors Corporation, 44, **150**
Chevron Corporation, 153
Chicago World's Fair. *See* World's Columbian Exposition of 1893
Chisholm, Boyd & White Company, 154
Chlorine Institute, 141
Chloromycetin, 94, 146
Chrysler Corporation, 44, **45**, 81, 142
CIM (computer-integrated manufacturing), 119, 122
Cincinnati Milacron Corporation, 121
CIO (Congress of Industrial Organization), 59, 144
Coca-Cola Company, The, 154
Cold War, 89
Collins, Michael, 107
Computer languages: COBOL, 98; FLOW-MATIC, 98; FORTRAN, 98
Computers, 85, **85**, 97, 98, **98**, 99, 112, 118, 121, 122, 123, **123**
ConAgra, Inc., 140
Conklin Instrument Corporation, 148
Conrad, Frank, 47
Construction Industry Manufacturing Association, 138
Continental Baking Company, 142, **142**, 143
Control Data Systems Inc., 112
Convair. *See* General Dynamics Convair Division
Coolidge, President Calvin, 43
Cooper Industries, 153
Corning Glass Works, 140
Crawford, Frederick, 50
Cray-1 supercomputer, 112
Credit card, 95, **95**
Crocker Research Labs, 142
Crown Cork & Seal Company, Inc., 141
CT (computer tomography). *See* CAT scan

D

Daisy Manufacturing Company, 148
Dana Corp., 137
Danco Metal Products, Inc., 145
Danforth, Robinson, 136
Dart & Kraft, 154
da Vinci, Leonardo, 65

Dayton Engineering Laboratories Company (Delco), 29
Deere & Company, 55
De Forest, Dr. Lee, 34, **34**, 49, 138, 141
Delco. *See* Dayton Engineering Laboratories Company
Deming, W. Edwards, 113, 132
Digital Equipment Corporation, 149
Disney Company, Walt, 144
Dodge, 139
Dolan, Thomas, 14
Domino Sugar Corp., 138
Donaldson Company, Inc., 140
Donnelly and Sons Co., R. R., **136**
Doolittle, Jimmy, 50
Douglas Aircraft. *See* McDonnell Douglas Corporation
Dow Chemical Company, 126, 147, 154
du Pont de Nemours Company, E. I., 60, **60**, **61**, 80, **80**, 81, 142, **142**, 144, 150; Cellophane, **87**, 142; Teflon, 81; *See also* Nylon; Rubber: synthetic rubber
Drucker, Peter, 133, 144
Duryea, Charles and Frank, 28, 136
Dynapac. *See* Svedala International

E

Earhart, Amelia, 50, 142
Eastman, George, 19, 93, 137, 142
Eastman Kodak Company, 19, **19**, 92, 93, 142, 144; Kodacolor film, 49
Eaton Corporation, 139, 155
Eaton, Joseph, 139
Eberhard Faber Co., 32
Eckert-Mauchly Computer Corporation, 147
Edison, Thomas A., 14, 65
Einstein, Albert, 111, 138
Eisenhower, President Dwight D., 109
Electric power, 8, 14, 15
Electronic Controls Co. (ECCO), 151, **152**
Elevator, 16, 17
Elgin Sweeper Company, 139, **139**
Emerson Electric Co., 15, **140**
ENIAC (Electronic Numerical Integrator and Computer), 85, **85**, 97, 98, 146
Ensign-Bickford Company, 144
Environmentally conscious manufacturing, 120, 126, 127
Erie Steel Construction Company, 139
ESCO (Electric Steel Foundry Company), 139, **151**
E&T Fairbanks Company, 136
Eveready Battery Company, 137, **140**, 141, **143**, 146, 148, 149, 153
Evinrude, Ole, 138

F

Fairey Aviation Company, 146
Fast food, 115
Faultless Rubber, 141
Featherstone, Harry, 131

Federal Paper Board Company, Inc., 147
Fessenden, Reginald A., 34, **34**, 137, 138
Fiber optics, 110, **110**, 119
Firestone Tire & Rubber Company, 29, 72
Flemming, Sir Alexander, 84
FONAR Corporation, 152
Food, packaged, 22, 23, **23**, 127
Ford, Henry, 26, 28, 29, 137, 138, 139, 140
Ford Motor Company, 44, 72, 76, 131, 137, 140, 141, 142; Model A, 44, 142; Model T, 28, **28**, 29, 44, 138, 142
Forestry, 126, **126**
Frigidaire, 48, **48**, 142
Frozen food, 66, **66**
Fry, Art, 64, **153**

G

Galvin Manufacturing Company. *See* Motorola
Geiger counter , 139
General Dynamics Corporation, 148; Convair Division, 50, **72**, **75**, 76, 101; USS *Nautilus*, 100, 147
General Electric Company, 36, 48, 76, 81, 108, 138, 139, 144, 148, 155
General Foods Corporation, 66; Birds Eye brand, 66, **66**, 142
General Mills Company, 142, 145
General Motors Corporation, 44, 72, 138, 144, 154
Genentech, Inc., 152
Genetic engineering, 120, 125
Gerber, Daniel, 142
Gibson Greetings, 155
Giddings & Lewis, Inc., **99**, 140, **154**
Gillette, King C., 18, **18**
Gillette Company, The, 18, **18**, 136
Glenshaw Glass Co., 155
Goddard, Professor Robert H., 27, 52, **52**, 142
Gompers, Samuel, 13
Goodrich Company, The BF, 53, 72, 80, 142, 146
Goodyear Tire & Rubber Co., 29, **29**, 136, 137
Gorgas, William C., 137
Great Depression, 43, 58, 60
Great Lakes Chemical Corporation, 143
Grove North America, 146
Grumman Corporation, 152
Gyroscope, 50

H

Hall, Charles Martin, 31, **31**, 138
Hallmark Cards, Inc., 139
Haloid Company. *See* Xerox Corporation
Hamilton Beach Manufacturing Company, 139
Hanna Co., M. A., 154
Hannay, Clifford B., 143
Hannay Reels, 143, **144**
Hansen, William, 67, **67**
Harding, President Warren G., 27

Harley-Davidson Inc., 137, **137**
Harris Corporation, 155
Harrison, Ross, 138
Hart, Schafner & Marx, 32
Hartley Co., Inc., 144
Heinz Company, H. J., 142
Helicopter, 65, **65**
Herman Miller, Inc., 147
Heroult, Paul-Louis-Toussaint, 31
Hertz Corporation, 44, 140
Hewlett-Packard, 111, 144, 151, 154
Highway construction, 109
Hoffman-LaRoche, Inc., 154
Holt, Benjamin, 55, 137
Hoover, President Herbert, 58
Hoover, William B., 36
Hoover Company, 36, 138
Hoover Dam, 59
Hoover vacuum cleaner, 148
Hopper, Grace, **98**
Hotpoint, 147
Houdry, Frederick Eugene Jules, 82
Hubble Space Telescope, 120, 128, **128**, 155
Hughes Danbury Optical Systems, Inc., 128
Hughes Research Laboratories, 111
Hussey Seating Company Inc., 154
Humphreys, Robert E., 139
Hyde Park Electronics, Inc., 149
Hydroelectric power, 14-15, **15**, 31, 136

I

IBM (International Business Machines Corporation), 65, 98, 143, 149; 701 computer, 98, 147; 752 computer, 98, 148; PC (personal computer), 112, 123, **123**, 153
I.C.I., 153
Indianapolis 500 race, 44
Industrial Safety Equipment Association, 143
Information superhighway, 119
Ingersoll-Rand Corporation, 32, 109, 136, **137**; Drillmaster, 109; Crawlmaster, 149
Ingram, E. W. "Billy", 115
Institute of Electrical and Electronics Engineers (IEEE), 153
Intel Corporation, 112, **112**, **150**, 151, 152, 154, 155
International Harvester, 55
International Mercantile Marine Company, 137
International Telecommunications Satellite Organization (Intelsat), 106

J

Jack-In-The-Box restaurant, 147
Jeep, 78
Jenny, William Le Baron, 16
Jervis B. Webb Company, 146
Jobs, Steven P., 112
Johnson, Martin, **49**
Johnson Controls, Inc., 154
Johnson & Johnson, 141
Jones & Laughlin Steel. *See* LTV Corporation
Jumbo jets. *See* Aviation
Just-in-time manufacturing, 113, **113**

K

Kaiser Company, Henry J., 79, **79**; Liberty ship production, 79, **79**, 145
Kaiser, Henry J., 79, 145
KDKA, 47, 141
Kellogg, Dr. John Harvey, 22
Kellogg, W. K., 22, **22**, 136
Kellogg Company, 22, 136, 137
Kettering, Charles F., 29, **29**, 139
Kevlar, 92, 151
KitchenAid, 148
Kiva Container Corp., 126, 147
Kipping, F. S., 137
Klystron, 67, **67**, 144
Kohler Co., 141, **141**, **146**

L

Labor organizations, 59, 118
Lackawanna Steel, **138**
Lakewood Manufacturing, 146
Land, Dr. Edwin H., 93, **93**, 142, 143, 146
Landa Systems, 150
Langley, Samuel, 30
LaPlant Choate Manufacturing Company, 141
Lasers, 111, **111**
La-Z-Boy Chair Company, 142
Lederle Laboratories, 94, 146
Leisure activities, 88, 89, 92
Lennox International Inc., 155
Lever Bros. Co., 136
Levi Strauss & Company, 147
Lilly & Company, Eli: Darvon, 94; Prozac, 124, **141**
Lincoln Electric Co., 136, 143, 155
Lindbergh, Charles A., **41**, 50, **51**, 52, 142
Lockheed Martin Corporation, 50, 128, 151, 152; L-1011, 108; P-38 Lightning, **77**
LTV Corporation, 150
Lukens Steel Company, 139, **145**

M

Machine tools, 15, 59, 85, 99
Maimann, Theodore, 111
Manhattan Project, 81, **81**, 100
Marconi, Guglielmo, 34, 136
Marion Merrell Dow Inc., 154
Marmon, 139
Marriott International, 44, 142
Maser, 111
Masking tape. *See* 3-M
MasterCard International, 95
Mattel, Inc., 148
Maytag Company, 36, 72, 139, 140
McDivitt, James A., 107
McDonald Manufacturing Company, A. Y., 148
McDonald's Corporation, 115, **115**, 147
McDonnell Douglas Corporation, 50, 62, **62**, 76, 144, 155; DC-3, 62, **62**, 144; DC-10, 108, 151
McGraw Electric Company, 36, 143
MCI, 153
McLuhan, Marshall, 90
Mead Corporation, 143
Medusa Corp., 155

Merck & Company, Inc., 124, 145;
Mevacor, 124
Microprocessor, 112, **112**, 119
Microsoft Corporation, 154
Microwave oven, 114, **114**
Miles Laboratories, 143
Miller Electric Manufacturing Company, 152
Minnesota Mining and Manufacturing Company. *See* 3M
Mobil Oil, 51, 149; Mobil Chemical Company, 149
Monroe Auto Equipment Company, 143
Monsanto Company, 125, 137; Newleaf potato plant, 125; Roundup, 125
Moore School of Electrical Engineering, 146
Morgan, J. P., 14, 137
Morgan, Dr. Paul, 60
Motion pictures, 35, **35**, **40**, 43, 49, **49**
Motorola Inc., 131, **131**
MRI (magnetic resonance imaging), 124
Multiplex Company, 138
Myers Co., F. E., 137

N

Nalco Chemical Company, 145
NASA (National Aeronautics and Space Administration), 101, 107, 111, 147, 153, 155; *Challenger*, 120; *Explorer I*, 101; *Freedom 7*, 107; Gemini 4, 107; *Pioneer II*, 107; Project Apollo, **103**, 105, 107; Project Gemini, 107; Project Mercury, 107, **149**; *Saturn V*, 52; *Viking I*, 107
National Association of Manufacturers (NAM), 13, 14, **14**, 32, 43, 70, 74, **74**, 136, 145, 147, 149, 151, 152, 153, 154, 155
National Biscuit Company, 136
National Industrial Council, 74
National Industries for the Blind, 144
National Screw Machine Products Association, 151
National Starch & Chemical Company, 136
National System of Interstate and Defense Highways, 109
Newport News Shipbuilding & Dry Dock Co., **39**, 79, **79**, 149, 153, 155, **155**; USS *Enterprise*, 79, 100; USS *Essex*, 79; USS *Hornet*, 79; USS *Intrepid*, 79; North Carolina Shipbuilding, 79, **79**; USS *Yorktown*, 79
Niagara Falls, 14, 31; *See also* hydroelectric power
Niagara Mohawk Power Corporation, 100, 147
Nixon, President Richard M., 107
North American Aviation, 76, 153; F-100 Super Sabre, 101; P-51 Mustang, 76
Northeast Electronic Company, 65
Northrop Grumman Corporation, 155
Nucor Corporation, 150
Numeric Controls, 85, 99, **99**
Nylon, 60, **60**, **61**, 144, 145; parachutes, **61**, 72

O

Office equipment, automated, 20, **20**, 21, **21**
Olds, Ransom E., 28; Mercury Oldsmobile, 28
Olin Corporation, 136
Oppenheimer, J. R., 81
Optical fibers. *See* Fiber optics
Oracle Systems Corporation, 152
OshKosh B'Gosh, Inc., **112**, 136
Otis Elevator Company, 16, **17**
Otis, Elisha Graves, 16
Outboard Marine Corporation, 142

P

Pabst, Karl, 78
Packard Motor Company, 139
Panama Canal, 32, **33**
Parke-Davis, 94, 146
Parker Hannifin Corporation, 50, 151
Parsons, Charles, 136
Peavey Electronics Corporation, **122**, 153, 155
Penicillin, 71, 72, 84, **84**, 94
Penney Company, Inc., J. C., 43
Pentair Corp., 137
Perkin-Elmer Corporation, 128
Petroleum industry, 29, 58, 82, 83
Pfizer Inc, 72, 84, 94, 145, 146; Procardia XL, 124; terramycin, 94
Pharmaceuticals, 71, 84, 94, 95, 124
Photocopy process. *See* xerography
Photography, 19, 49; instant, 93
Pipelines, 83; *See also* Trans-Alaskan
Pitt-Des Moines, Inc., 145
Pittsburgh Reduction Company. *See* Alcoa
Plastics: thermoplastics, 32, **32**; PVC, 53, **53**; synthetic fibers, 60, **60**, **61**
Polaroid products, 93, 142, 143
Pope, Alexander A., 28
Post, C. W., 22, 136
Post-it. *See* 3-M
Postum Cereal Company, 22, 136, 142
PPG Industries, 44, 142, 153
Pratt & Whitney Aircraft, 108
Premark International, Inc., 154
Proctor & Gamble Company, The, 90, **144**
Pure Oil. *See* Unocal Corporation
PVC (polyvinyl chloride), 53, **53**

R

Radar, 34, 67, 72, 90, 114
Radio, 34, 42, 47, 49
Radiotherapy, 67; *See also* CAT scan
Railroad, 63
Ralston Purina Company, 136
Ramsay, William, 136
Raytheon Manufacturing Company, 72, 114, **114**, 147, 155; magnetron, 72, 114;
Radarange, 114, **114**
RCA Corporation, 47, 90, **97**, 98, 140, 141, 143, 144, 145, **145**, 148
Reagan, President Ronald, 119, 153
Reed Exhibition Company, 149, 155
Reedrill, Inc., 145
Remington-Rand, 20, **20**, 21
Reynolds Metals Company, 146

Rhyne Lumber Company, 141
Robinson Industries, Inc., 136
Rocco Enterprises, Inc., 126, **127**, 144, 154
Rockefeller, John D., 58
Rocketry, 27, 52
Roosevelt, President Franklin D., 58, 76
Roosevelt, President Theodore, 26, 137
Ross, Ronald, 136
Rubber, 44, 71; neoprene, **80**; synthetic rubber, 80, **80;** tire industry, 29
Rubber Manufacturers Association, 140, 142
Rubbermaid, 143
Rutherford, Ernest, 136

S

Sabin, Dr. Albert, 95
Salk, Dr. Jonas E., **94**, 95, **95**
Sandmeyer Steel Company, 147, **147**
Sara Lee, 149
Satellites, 52, 106, **106**, 119
Schawlow, Arthur, 111
Schering-Plough, 154
Schick, Inc., 141
Scotch-tape. *See* 3M
Sears, Roebuck and Co., 43
Seldon, George B., 136
Semon, Dr. Waldo, 53
Shady Brook Farms. *See* Rocco Enterprises, Inc.
Shanklin, Edward, 16
Sharp Electronics Corp., 151
Shepard, Alan B., Jr., 107
Sherwin-Williams Company, 72, **73,** 143
Shipbuilding, 39, 78
Shockley, William, 97
Sikorsky, Igor, 65, **65**, 139, 145
Skyscrapers, 16, **17**
Sloan, Alfred P., 44
Sly Inc., 136
Small manufacturers, 88, 100, 126-127
Snap-On Tools Incorporated, 140
Snorkel Economy, 148
Sony Electronics Inc., 149, 151, 155
Space exploration, 52, 101, 107, 128
Spencer, Percy LeBaron, 72, 114
Spengler, Murray, 36, 138
Sperry, Elmer, 50, **50**, 138, 143, **138**
Sperry Gyroscope Company, 50, **50**, 138
Sperry Rand, 98, 148
Spicer, Clarence, 137
Spicer Manufacturing Company. *See* Dana Corp.
Spirit of St. Louis, **41**, 50, **51**, 142
Sputnik, 101
Stainless steel, 63
Standard Oil, 29, 137, 139
Stanley Steamer, 136
Stanley Works, The, 145, 155
Steel: construction, 16, 26, 32; stainless, 63
Steel Shipping Container Institute, 145
Steiff, Richard, 137
Stone Construction Equipment, 150
Stone Container Corporation, 142
Stora Newton Falls, 136
Storage Technology Corporation, 150
Stow Manufacturing Company, 155
Streptomycin, 84

Studebaker Automobile Company, 139
Sun Company, Inc. (Sun Oil Company) **44**, 82, 144, 146
Sunbeam Corporation, 143
Superior Technical Ceramics, 136
Svedala International, 147
Swanson, Gloria, **49**
Syntex, 94, 147, **148**
Synthetic light polarizer, 93

T

Taylor, Frederick, 26, 139
Taylor Machine Works, 142
Taylor-Wharton Iron & Steel Company, 140
Teflon. *See* Du Pont
Telecommunications, 43, 46, 106, 110
Television, 34, 88, 90, **90**, **91**, 136
Telstar, 106, **106**
Tenneco Inc., 83, **83**, 145, 150, 152, 154, 155
Tennessee Gas and Transmission Company. *See* Tenneco Inc.
Terramycin, 94, 146
Tesla, Nikola, 14
Texas Instruments Inc., 150
Thomson, J. J., 136
3M, 64, 126, 142, 143, 152, **153**; masking tape, 64, **64**; Post-it, 64; Scotch tape, 064, 143
Timken Company, The, **2-3**, 136, 140, 153, 155, **155**
Toledo-Commutator, 136
Torbensen, Viggio, 139
Torbensen Gear and Axle Company, 139
Townes, Charles H., 111
Total quality management, 113, 132
Tractors, 54, 55, 78
Trans-Alaskan pipeline, **152**
Transatlantic telephone cable, 46, **46**
Transistor, 34, 97, **97**, 98, 112
Traulsen & Co., 144
Trinova Corporation, 154
Triode vacuum tube, 34, **34**
Trowbridge, Alexander B., 153
Truman, President Harry S., 100
TRW, 50
Typewriter, 20, **20**, 21, **21**, 65, **65**

U

Una-dyn (Universal Dynamics Inc.), 126, **127**
Underwood Typewriter Company, **20**, 21
Unions. *See* Labor organizations
United Aluminum Corporation, 136
United States Steel (USX Corporation), 26, 137
UNIVAC, 98, **98**
Unocal Corporation, **82**, 137
Upjohn Company, 154
Upton Machine Co. *See* Whirlpool Corporation

V

Vacuum Oil Company, 82
Vacuum tubes, 34, 98
Van Rooy Coffee Co., 143

Vanderbilt, William K., 14
Varian, Russell and Sigurd, 67, **67**, 144
Varian Associates, 67, 144, **146**, 147
Vaughn-Bassett Furniture Co., 136
Verbatim Corporation, 126, 151
Vought-Sikorsky Aircraft Company, 65, **65**

W

Waksman, Selman, 84
Walker Manufacturing Company, 143
Warner Brothers, 142
Webster, Professor David, 67, **67**
Western Cartridge Company, 136
Western Electric. *See* AT&T
Westinghouse Electric Company, 14, 47, 48, 81, 136, 141, 148
Westvaco Corporation, 126, **127**, 149, 153, 155
WGY, 142
Whirlpool Corporation, 139
White, Edward H. II, 107
Will-Burt Company, The, 131
Wilson, President Woodrow, 27, 46
Witherow, William, 70
Witt Company, The, 126, **126**, 136
Woodyard, John, 67, **67**
Woolworth, F. W., 43, 139, 144
World's Columbian Exposition of 1893, 8-9, **8**, **9**, 12-13
World War I, 27, 30, 31; and radio, 34, 47; and the tractor, 55; wartime production, **25**, 27, 31, 39, **39**, women in the workforce, 39, 75
World War II, 52, 62, 76, 78, 79, 80, 81, 82, 88; wartime production, 60, **61**, 70-71, 72, **72**, **73**, 74, **78**, **79**, 80, 83, 84; women in the workforce, **68**, **69**, 71, 74, 75, **75**
Worthington Industries, Inc., 148, 153
Worzalla Publishing Company, 155
Wozniak, Stephen G., 112
Wright brothers, 27, 30, **30**, 31, 137, 138

X

Xerox Corporation, 96, **96**, 144, 146, 148, 151
Xerography, 96

Y

Yeager, Capt. Charles E. "Chuck", 101, **101**
Yeager Industries, Inc., 149
York Wallcoverings, 136

Z

Zephyr, 63, **63**, 143
Zippers, 139
Zsigmondy, R. A., 137
Zworykin, Vladimir K., **90**, 141, 143, **145**

Bold listings indicate illustrated material

Following is a list of companies whose trademarked products are mentioned in this book:

Alza Corp. — Testoderm; Amana Refrigeration Inc. — Radarange; American Can — Dixie; American Cyanamid Co. — Aureomycin; American Express Co. — American Express; Amgen — Epogen; AMP Inc. — Action Pin Contacts; Apple Computer Inc. — Apple II, Macintosh; AT&T — Touch Tone; Bamerilease, Inc. — BankAmericard; Bausch & Lomb Inc. — Ray-Ban; Boeing Co. — 747, 737; Campbell Soup Co. — Campbell's; Citicorp Diners Club Inc. — Diners Club; Cray Research Inc. — Cray; The Eastman Kodak Co. — Brownie, Kodachrome, Kodacolor, Kodak; E. I. du Pont de Nemours & Co., Inc. — Antron, Dacron, Kevlar, Lycra, Teflon; Eli Lilly & Co. — Darvon, Prozac; Ensign-Bickford Industries Inc. — Primacord; Eveready Battery Co. — Energizer; Formica Corp. — Formica; General Dynamics — Atlas; General Mills Co. — Cheerios; Georgia-Pacific Resins, Inc. — Bakelite; Gerber Products Co. — Gerber; Hewlett-Packard Co. — Deskjet; Hoechst Celanese Corp. — Fortrel; Hoffman-LaRoche Inc. — Roferon; Hoover — Hoover; Ingersoll-Rand Co. — Crawlmaster, Drillmaster; Intel Corp. — Intel, Pentium; International Business Machines Corp. — Selectric; ITT Continental Baking Co. — Hostess, Twinkies, Wonder; Johnson & Johnson — Band-Aids; Kellogg Co. — Kellogg's Corn Flakes; KitchenAid Inc. — KitchenAid; Kraft General Foods, Inc. — Birds Eye, Grape Nuts, Postum; La-Z-Boy Chair Co. — La-Z-Boy; Lotus Development Corp. — Lotus Notes; Marion Merrell Dow Pharmaceuticals Inc. — Seldane; MasterCard International Inc. — MasterCard; Mattel, Inc. — Barbie; McDonald's Corp. — Big Mac, Egg McMuffin, McDonalds; McDonnell Douglas Corp. — DC-10; McGraw-Edison Co. — Toastmaster; Merck & Co. Inc — Mevacor; Microsoft Corp. — Windows; Miles Inc. — Alka-Seltzer; Monsanto Co. — NewLeaf, Roundup; Pfizer Inc — Procardia XL; Pfizer Inc — Terramycin; Polaroid Corp. — Polaroid; PPG Industries, Inc. — Duplate; Ralston Purina Co. — Beech Nut; Reynolds Metals Co. — Reynolds Wrap; Richardson-Vicks Inc. — Vaporub; Rohm & Hass Co. — Plexiglas; Schering Corp. — Intron; The Seven-Up Co. — 7-Up; Sony Corp. — Trinitron; Sterling Drug Inc. — Novocain; Sunbeam Corp. — Mixmaster; 3M — Post-it, Scotch; Unisys — UNIVAC; The Upjohn Co. — Rogaine; Varian Associates Inc. — Clinac; Visa International Service Association — VisaCard; Warner-Lambert Co. — Chloromycetin; Westvaco Corp. — Nuchar, Printkote; White Castle System Inc. — White Castle; Xerox Corp. — Xerox;

Photo Credits

t = top b = bottom l = left r = right o = opposite

Alabama Laser Technologies, 111-l; Aluminum Company of America (Alcoa), 31; American Automobile Manufacturers Assn., endpapers, 28, 139-l, 150-l; American Express Company, 95-r; AT&T Archives, 46-t, 110, 150-r; Amgen Inc., cover, 3, 117 ©Bill Varie 1988; AMP Inc., 151; The Bancroft Library, University of California, 79-b; Bell & Howell Company, 49-r; The Bettmann Archive, 19, 20-r, 30-t, 32-t, 34-b, 41, 46-b, 49-l, 91, 106, 152-r; The BFGoodrich Company, 53; The Boeing Company, 30-b, 76, 108; Brown Brothers, 37, 47; Brunswick Corporation, 92; Campbell Soup Company, 11, 23; Carrier Corporation, 35; Carton Service, Incorporated, 122-t; Case Corporation, 54-t, 55, 78-t, 78-br; Caterpillar Inc., 54-b; Chrysler Corporation, 45, 121; The Cincinnati Historical Society, 14; R. R. Donnelly and Sons Co., 136; The E.I. du Pont de Nemours Company, 80, 142-l; Electronic Controls Co., 152-l; Elgin Sweeper Company, 139-r; Emerson Electric Co., 140-r; Federal Paper Board Company, Inc., 128; Frozen Food Age Magazine, 66-r; General Dynamics Convair Division, 69, 72, 75; General Motors Research Library, 29-t; Giddings & Lewis, Inc., 99, 154-r; The Gillette Company, 18; Goodyear Tire and Rubber Company, 29-bl; Hagley Museum and Library, 15, 20-l, 25, 29-br, 36, 38, 39-r, 48, 50, 57, 60, 61, 65-r, 74, 85, 87, 98, 138, 145-r; Hannay Reels, 144-r; Harley-Davidson Inc., 137-t; Hughes Danbury Optical Systems, Inc., 130; IBM, 65-l, 123; Ingersoll-Rand, 137-bl; Intel Corporation, 112; Kellogg Company, 22; Kohler Company, 141-r; Library of Congress, 16, 21-t, 33; Eli Lilly & Company, 141-l; Lockheed Corporation, 77, 154-l; McDonald's Corporation 115; McDonnell-Douglas, 62; Mobil Corporation, 51; Monsanto Company, 125; NASA, 103, 107; Nebraska State Historical Society, 63; Newport News Shipbuilding, 39-l, 79-t, 100, 155-l; OshKosh B'Gosh, Inc., 113; Otis Elevator Company, 17-r; Peavey Electronics Corp., 122-b; Pfizer Inc, 84; The Proctor & Gamble Company, 144-l; Ralston Purina Company, 22-b, 140-l, 142-r, 143-l; Rocco Enterprises, Inc., 127-t; The Sherwin-Williams Company, 73, 143-r; Sun Company Inc., 44; Tenneco Inc., 83; 3M, 64, 153; The Timken Company, 2-3, 155-l; UPI/Bettmann, 17-l, 34-l, 52, 66-l, 81, 90, 93, 94, 95-l, 97, 101, 109, 111-r, 114, 145-l; Universal Dynamics, 127-b; Varian Associates, 67, 124; Westvaco Corporation, 129; The Witt Company 126; Xerox Corporation, cover, 96.

Special Credits

p. 8: Lithograph; ICHi-25185; All the nations are welcome...; World's Columbian Exposition, Chicago (Ill.); 1893; Creator unknown; courtesy of the Chicago Historical Society; **p. 9:** Lithograph; ICHi-02347; The Ferris wheel, midway pleasance...; World's Columbian Exposition, Chicago (Ill.); 1893; Artist — after a painting by Charles Graham; courtesy of the Chicago Historical Society; **p. 10:** Thomas Pollock Anshutz, detail of *The Ironworkers' Noontime*, 1880. Oil on canvas, 17-1/8" x 24" © The Fine Arts Museums of San Francisco. Gift of Mr. and Mrs. John D. Rockefeller 3rd, 1979.7.4 ; **p. 24:** Diego M. Rivera, detail of *The Detroit Industry*, North Wall, 1932-1933. Fresco, 33.10.N. Photograph © The Detroit Institute of Arts, Detroit, Michigan, 1995. Gift of Edsel B. Ford; **p. 40:** © Michael Puig; **p. 56:** National Museum of Art, Washington, D.C./Art Resource, New York, S0077248, 1965.18.11,12,13, Color Transp.Gropper, William. Detail of *Construction of the Dam* (mural study, Department of the Interior, National Park Service) 1937. National Museum of American Art, Washington, D.C., USA; **p. 68:** Norman Rockwell, detail of *Rosie the Riveter*, 3/29/43. Printed by permission of the Norman Rockwell Family Trust, © 1943 the Norman Rockwell Family Trust. Transparency courtesy of the Curtis Archives; **p. 86:** Thomas Hart Benton, detail of *Fluid Catalytic Crackers*, 1945. Oil on canvas mounted on masonite 58" by 69". Courtesy of MIT List Visual Arts Center, Cambridge, Massachusetts. Gift of Standard Oil of New Jersey, 1951.001; **p. 102:** Tony Ligamari, detail of *Label Painting*, a collage of scanner bar-code labels, work in progress, 65" x 118", reproduced by permission of the artist; **p. 116:** Peter Max, detail of *Made in America*, 1995. Peter Max, one of the most renowned artists of our time, created *Made in America* to celebrate U.S. manufacturers' myriad contri-butions of world-class products for our society. From the automobile to the computer chip, American-made products have improved our standard of living and been the benchmark of innovation and quality around the globe. One of four images created by Peter Max to celebrate 100 years of manufacturing excellence, *Made in America* joins a host of patriotic works by the visionary pop artist.

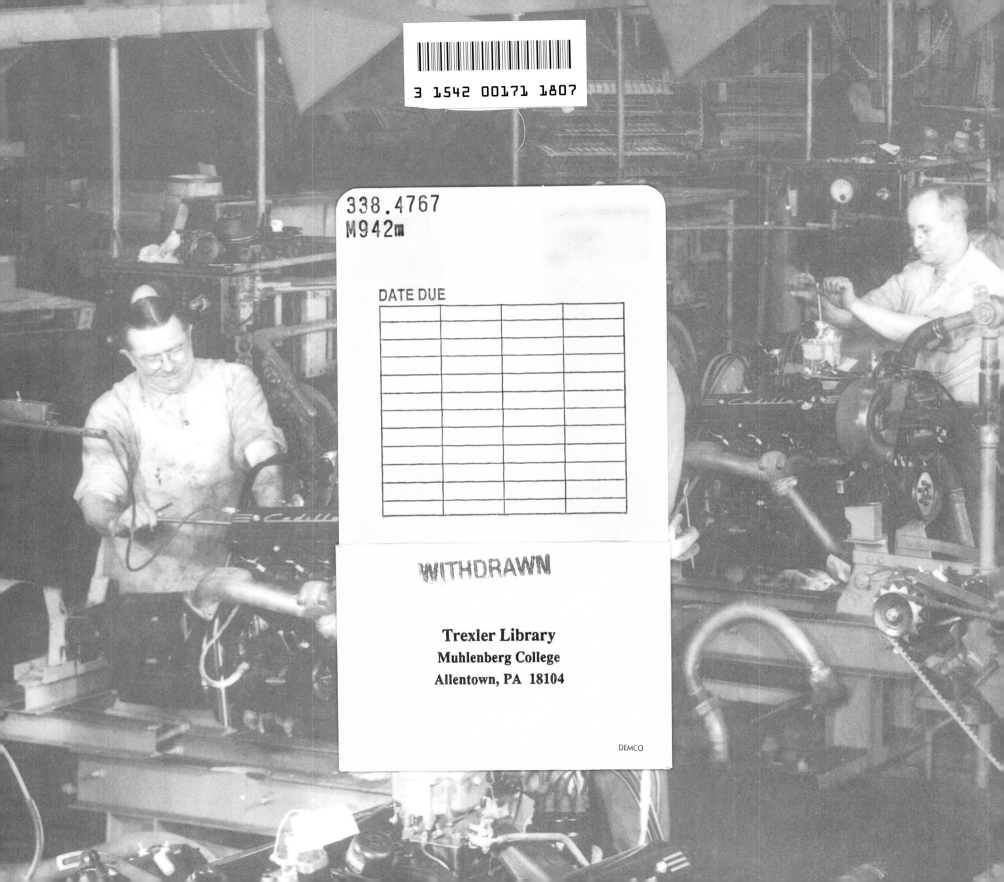